Progressing Performance and Well-being at Work

NEW HORIZONS IN MANAGEMENT

Series Editor: Professor Sir Cary Cooper, *50th Anniversary Professor of Organizational Psychology and Health at Alliance Manchester Business School, University of Manchester, UK and President of the Chartered Institute of Personnel and Development and British Academy of Management.*

This important series makes a significant contribution to the development of management thought. This field has expanded dramatically in recent years and the series provides an invaluable forum for the publication of high quality work in management science, human resource management, organizational behaviour, marketing, management information systems, operations management, business ethics, strategic management and international management.

The main emphasis of the series is on the development and application of new original ideas. International in its approach, it will include some of the best theoretical and empirical work from both well-established researchers and the new generation of scholars.

For a full list of Edward Elgar published titles, including the titles in this series, visit our website at www.e-elgar.com.

Progressing Performance and Well-being at Work

Travelling the Loop

Jaap Paauwe

Professor of Organization and Human Resource Management, Department of Human Resource Studies, Tilburg University, the Netherlands

NEW HORIZONS IN MANAGEMENT

Edward Elgar
PUBLISHING

Cheltenham, UK • Northampton, MA, USA

Published by
Edward Elgar Publishing Limited
The Lypiatts
15 Lansdown Road
Cheltenham
Glos GL50 2JA
UK

Edward Elgar Publishing, Inc.
William Pratt House
9 Dewey Court
Northampton
Massachusetts 01060
USA

A catalogue record for this book
is available from the British Library

Library of Congress Control Number: 2024934593

This book is available electronically in the **Elgar**online
Business subject collection
http://dx.doi.org/10.4337/9781800377943

ISBN 978 1 80037 793 6 (cased)
ISBN 978 1 80037 794 3 (eBook)

Printed and bound by CPI Group (UK) Ltd, Croydon, CR0 4YY

Contents

Figures

Tables

About the author

Jaap Paauwe is an Emeritus Professor of Organization and Human Resource Management at Tilburg University. His research focuses on the relationship between HRM, performance and well-being, HR functional excellence, HRM and the institutional context, HR analytics and Talent Management. From 2014–2018, he was the acting Vice-Dean for Research at Tilburg School of Social and Behavioural Sciences. Right now, he is involved in a nationwide initiative for a new approach towards recognizing talents, strengths, and career possibilities for academics. He initiated the People Management Center, a Center for Work, Well-being and Performance, which focuses on building bridges between academia and practitioners, for which he is still active. Jaap holds an honorary chair at Pablo de Olavide University in Sevilla (Spain) and an honorary chair at North-West University in Potchefstroom (South-Africa). He has published widely on the aforementioned topics in international refereed journals and books. He is involved in a range of executive training programs at various business schools, among which are TIAS and FHR Lim-A-Po Institute (Surinam), for which he has recently been appointed as Convenor for the strategic HRM program. His latest book, written together with Elaine Farndale, has been published under the title: *HRM, Strategy and Performance: A Contextual Approach*, Oxford University Press, 2017.

Website: https://research.tilburguniversity.edu/en/persons/jaap-paauwe

Preface

For more than 35 year I have been active in the field of employment relations and Human Resource Management. The first 10 years of my career I worked in business and for the trade union movement, then, and since 1988, I have worked as an academic at several universities (both in the Netherlands and abroad). I have always kept in mind that the field of Human Resource Studies is an applied academic discipline. Those who teach, study, and do research in that domain benefit from close contact with practitioners and the main stakeholders in this area, such as organizations (both profit and non-profit), government, trade unions, and professional bodies. As academic researchers and tutors, we cannot do a proper job without close interactions with all these stakeholders. They are on top of new issues and challenges (for example the gig or platform economy, digital transformation of work, etc.), and they also have the data we need for our research. Data we collect through case-studies, survey research, machine-generated data, and which help us to do a proper piece of academic research to advance the fields of employment relations (ER) and human resource management (HRM).

The next step is to publish about these findings, which we mainly do in academic international refereed journals. These are all excellent journals, yet practitioners hardly read them simply because these papers are too difficult to read, or it just takes too much time in relationship with a pressing business agenda.

Having greatly benefitted throughout my academic career from close interaction with practitioners, companies, governmental bodies, trade unions, and practitioners (very often through their participation in executive training programs, for which I acted as their tutor), I increasingly feel the need to give them back something. What could be more precious for practitioners and our students – as future to be practitioners – to give them an overview of what our field of HR-Studies has achieved in terms of 'proven' findings of what really works in practice? Some of my colleagues might say 'Jaap, the field of HR Studies is not like Science, it all depends on the specific nature of an organization, sector and/or country'. Having been involved myself in the importance and development of a contextually-based Human Resource theory (Paauwe, 2004; Paauwe & Farndale, 2017), I am fully aware of the risky nature of my endeavour. However, I do have the optimistic perspective that we have a number of theories and HRM techniques, or interventions, which – let's say – work in 80% of the cases. This book is meant to present an overview of these, not all of course, but some major ones related to recruiting, selecting, motivating, and developing workers from a manager's actionable perspective. A manager who takes into account a proper balance between performance and well-being. After all, next to performing, we all want to get some sense of meaning, fairness, and fun out of work.

REFERENCES

Paauwe, J. (2004). *HRM and Performance: Achieving Long-term Viability*. Oxford: Oxford University Press Inc.
Paauwe, J., & Farndale, E. (2017). *Strategy, HRM and Performance: A Contextual Approach*. Oxford: Oxford University Press.

Acknowledgments

The majority of this book was written during my sabbatical leave at the School of Labor and Employment Relations (LER) at Pennsylvania State University in the USA. The facilities over there were excellent (even including a bike for commuting), thanks to my host Dr Elaine Farndale. I was based in a meeting room with a desk and an oval table and every week I added a draft chapter in print to the table, knowing that once the circle was completed, the book would be finished. A stimulating work setting.

Before starting with the writing process, I had discussions about the idea and intention of the book with colleagues and good friends such as Riccardo Peccei, David Guest, Paul Boselie, and Paul Jansen. Their advice, albeit varying, was not only stimulating but also valuable, and helped me to make up my mind about the target group, nature, and content of the book. As the book's main audience will be practitioners, I also presented a preliminary overview of the goals and intended content of the book to a group of Chief HR officers of large organizations, who applauded my effort. Next, I would like to thank Fleur Herben, our student assistant, for helping me with the literature search and all the editing requirements (APA style), and making sure that we would get permission for the figures.

Finally, my thanks to Francine O'Sullivan, Publisher, of Edward Elgar Publishing, who never lost her patience. Finalizing the book was quite a challenge due to the COVID-19 pandemic and the resulting emphasis upon other priorities. So, it took me longer than expected to finalize the book, but she always remained supportive.

1. Travelling the loop: an introduction and overview of content

This book presents a number of 'proven' Human Resource Management (HRM) techniques, practices and related theoretical insights, all with the aim of increasing and reflecting on the challenge of improving performance and well-being. Included is a range of theoretical insights which might, at first instance, contradict the relevance of writing a book from a manager's actionable perspective. However, that is not the case. On the contrary, presenting theoretical frameworks, which give insight into the underlying mechanisms and processes, will help a manager (as well as employees) to better understand what is going on and the reasons why. Five different questions have guided our selection of theoretical insights and related HRM techniques/practices in order to progress well-being and performance at work in a practical way.

1. WHY IS THE HRM SYSTEM AS IT IS?

This question concerns the shaping – the genesis – of HR practices and interventions. Which factors are accountable for the way HR practices have developed in a specific organization, sector and/or country? This is the domain of theories that account for and provide insight into the important role of context. Context, in this respect, can imply the market or sector, the technology being used and the educational level of the workforce, but also the institutional setting as far as legislation and the power of trade unions is concerned, as well as the culture of the sector. Two theories will be highlighted in this respect:

- *Institutional theory*, which is mainly focused on the impact at sectoral and country levels.
- *Contextually-based Human Resource theory* (Paauwe, 2004; Paauwe & Farndale, 2017), which brings all the relevant contextual factors together.

This framework integrates the different strands of theorizing both from a strategic management perspective (competition, market) as well as from a more institutional perspective (legislation, rules, traditions, values), and focuses on aligning added value (performance) and moral values such as well-being, fairness, and legitimacy – all being important criteria in the realm of HRM.

The framework enables a customized approach to the development of specific HRM practices, which help to solve the challenges concerning your workforce.

Offering these insights will help the reader and practitioner to get a better feel for the conditions, which impact the shaping of HR practices and why they differ per organization, per sector, and per country.

2.   WHY DO HRM PRACTICES WORK? EITHER FOR PERFORMANCE OR FOR WELL-BEING OR FOR BOTH!

Based on the focus of our book, this is probably the most important question, asking about the effects of HRM practices and interventions. We will be dealing with numerous practices, which have proven to be effective. Yet, there are also – at a higher level of abstraction – theoretical frameworks accounting for it. Three theories figure quite prominently in this respect:

- *AMO theory*, which is one of the most applied theories in the domain of HRM and especially useful from a line manager's perspective as it focuses on how to improve the Abilities, Motivation and Opportunity to participate for employees.
- *Goal-setting theory and feedback* relates very strongly to one of the core practices within HRM systems: performance management, which is the whole cycle of goal setting, monitoring, feedback, consequences for reward, and career development.
- *Human capital and the differentiated approach to employees*. Human capital consists of the knowledge, information, ideas, skills, and health of individuals and how these contribute to performance and competitive advantage.

3.   HOW CAN WE DEVELOP A MEANINGFUL WORK EXPERIENCE?

Once we know why HR practices do what they are supposed to do, we can help to make them even more effective. After all, HRM practices are not the 'silver bullet'. They need to be embedded. But embedded in what? Generally speaking, the effects of HRM practices are highly dependent on leadership and climate. Disrespectful leadership and the lack of a trusted climate will make almost any HRM practice powerless, irrespective of how advanced it might be. Luckily, the knowledge domains of HRM and organizational behaviour (OB) have developed important pieces of theorizing to help us to create 'strong' – in the sense of supporting the effectiveness of HR practices – situations. The following approaches will be dealt with:

* *Strengths of the HR system*: making sure that employees get the right and consistent signals about what the organization values and wants to achieve for their customers and/or clients and how HRM practices can be of help in this respect.
* *Well-being*: the crucial link between HRM practices and outcomes such as performance, commitment, enthusiasm, and job satisfaction.
* *Line-management enactment*: stimulating line managers to take on HRM responsibilities in co-creation with the HR function and employees.

4.   HOW CAN WE CREATE AN ENABLING WORK SETTING?

Work can be quite demanding, but in some cases, it can also be very boring through a lack of challenge, lack of autonomy, or lack of variation. When work is demanding, people feel challenged and involved, but once it becomes too demanding it can also act as a source of stress, including the risk of burnout in the long run. So, we need to create work situations, in which the job people carry out is surrounded by 'resources' which support the job holder and ensure that work is not too demanding. Or, in the case of boring, a highly repetitive job is changed into a job which offers a sufficient degree of quality of work and challenge. The following frameworks will provide insights into how to create a resource-rich and enabling work situation:

* *Job Demands Resources theory*. The Job Demands Resources (JDR) theory explains the interaction between job demands (such as work pressure) and job resources (e.g., support from your manager) and how that can result either in strain, stress, burn-out, or in positive outcomes such as feeling motivated, engaged etc. The focus is on improving both performance and employee well-being.
* *Job design and job crafting* relate to 'the content and organization of one's work activities, relationships, and responsibilities' (Parker, 2014, p. 662). Job crafting as part of job design involves the shaping of jobs by employees themselves. Job design and crafting are important topics for a (HR) manager. The characteristics of a job in terms of variety, autonomy, etc., impact individual outcomes such as satisfaction, health, and well-being, and at the organizational level, outcomes such as staff turnover and labour productivity.
* *Psychological contract theory* considers the employment relationship as an exchange relationship. The parties involved have their perceptions of

the kind of reciprocal promises and obligations in that relationship. Parties might differ on to what degree these promises are being delivered (*fulfillment* of the psychological contract, resulting in commitment and increased job performance) or to what degree the implicit promises have been *broken* or violated, with all kind of negative consequences both for the employee and the organization.

- *Psychological safety.* Taking care of a psychological safe work setting is important as it will be beneficial for learning and performance. People will more easily voice ideas, be more open to feedback, are willing to collaborate, take risks and dare to experiment.

5. DID WE DO A GOOD JOB?

In hindsight, we need to reflect on whether we did a good job as a manager in selecting and implementing our HR practices, in creating strong and resource rich situations, which hopefully have optimized both performance and well-being. The following two theories can help us to evaluate – to reflect – upon what we did:

- *Organizational justice* focuses on how employees perceive and judge the way they are treated by their organization, especially from an ethical and moral perspective. This will subsequently result (if positive) in responses, such as satisfaction, trust, commitment, job performance, helping colleagues, customer satisfaction and intention to leave. Paying attention to justice or fairness is thus very important for an organization and its line management as it has consequences for the quality of the employment relationship and its outcomes in terms of well-being and performance.
- *Social determination theory.* What do people want to get out of work? The theory distinguishes three basic needs: autonomy, belonging, and competency/mastery. These three needs form necessary ingredients, which drive the behaviour of individuals. The way in which work is organized, the behaviour of managers and colleagues, leadership style, and culture are all very important and influential for creating a context in which these basic needs are either worn down or nourished.

6. BUILT IN SAFEGUARDS

Presenting a range of chapters in this way might easily result in criticism that the specifics of all these different approaches have not been taken sufficiently into account, due to the word limit of each chapter and the promise to the readership to be concise. Well, this has been dealt with by including a list of references for further reading for those who want to know all the specifics.

Another point of possible criticism is the degree to which we have sufficiently considered the different circumstances and contingencies in which a theory – a practice – will or will not work? Doing that concisely is almost impossible. To respond to that kind of critique, we have made sure to select HR practices and related theories that have been proven to work in, let's say, 80% of cases, and we have included some safeguards to mitigate against the other 20%.

What are these safeguards? First of all, we refer to the Evidence-Based Management (EBM) approach, which has been outlined in a separate chapter/appendix at the end of this book. The Evidence-Based Management approach distinguishes four sources of information before being able to take a justified and solid decision in a specific situation, which are depicted in the following scheme by the Center for Evidence-Based Management (2011):

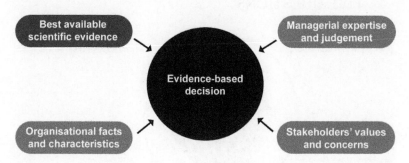

Note: Reprinted from the Center for Evidence-Based Management (CEBMa), 2011 (https://cebma.org)

Figure 1.1   The Evidence-Based Management (EBM) approach

In the following chapters, we only present *one out of the four* required sources as depicted in Figure 1.1, i.e., the source of 'best available scientific evidence'. Every chapter will include the core of the theory and related evidence as well as possibilities for application/intervention. It is up to the reader to take care of the other three sources (organizational facts/characteristics, values/concern of stakeholders, and his/her own expertise and judgement). In this way, allowing for a properly informed decision-making process in a specific situation. We refer to the appendix on Evidence-Based Management to get yourself acquainted with this approach and the kind of steps needed to make sure that all possible evidence and information is available before opting for a certain intervention in your organization.

As a second safeguard, a proven framework is presented in Chapter 3, which will help managers to develop a customized approach for their organization. The contextually-based Human Resource Theory (CBHRT) has been developed over the course of many years and explored and tested in more than 1000 different organizations, be it large, small, private, public, etc. The framework (Paauwe, 2004; Paauwe & Farndale, 2017) offers a customized approach, analysing the specific external and internal context and aligning both added and moral values. The framework therefore helps to shape your HRM system in a unique way and thus contributes to a sustained competitive advantage. Moreover, this framework includes an approach to take into account the other three sources of data (i.e., organizational data, stakeholders, and the professional expertise of practitioners) as highlighted by the EBM approach.

7.   IN CONCLUSION: TRAVELLING THE LOOP: THE FIVE QUESTIONS

Figure 1.2   Travelling the loop: the five questions

REFERENCES

Paauwe, J. (2004). *HRM and Performance: Achieving Long-term Viability.* Oxford: Oxford University Press.
Paauwe, J., & Farndale, E. (2017). *Strategy, HRM and Performance: A Contextual Approach.* Oxford: Oxford University Press.

2. The institutional perspective: how market, society, and organization interact[1]

TRIGGER

Imagine a management trainee from a European-based multinational company staying for a while as a trainee in a subsidiary, based in New York State. She will be surprised about the amount of authority managers have, the lack of discussion when giving a command and no real participation. New York State is also known for the so-called 'employment at will'. Without giving any notice and without the need to give a reason one can be dismissed immediately. Likewise, an employee may terminate his or her employment at any time. The situation on the other side of the ocean in mainland Europe will be totally different. A management trainee recruited at one of the USA-based subsidiaries and heading to the Netherlands for working a while at corporate headquarters will be surprised about the degree of discussion and participation in decision-making between management and workers, both informal as well as formal (via the works council). As far as dismissal is concerned, strict legislation requires notice periods and valid reasons for dismissal. Also, the employee him or herself is required to take into account a proper notice period, very often dependent on the length of service.

1. DEFINING THE CONCEPT AND HOW IT CAN HELP PRACTITIONERS

From a management perspective, one might consider organizations and related HRM practices as formally rational instruments to realize clearly defined objectives, such as increasing sales, rendering services, developing a new delivery channel. However, organizations are also driven by emotion and tradition, while being infused with values, habits, routines, and traditions from their wider environment. Institutional theory focuses on the non-rationality of processes at all levels in society whereby people and organizations conform to these social and cultural influences *without thinking* (Lammers et al., 2000).

'Without thinking' in this sense, means that these normative influences are *taken for granted* (Zucker, 1977). For example, considering getting married for the first time as an institution implies – as a taken for granted norm – that the bride with an almost 100% likelihood will wear a white dress.

Institutional theory, with its focus on the role and influence of values, traditions, and norms, offers important clues towards understanding external forces and how HRM practices evolve, change, and respond to these. Moreover, HRM professionals themselves are also subject to institutional pressures. Their values, vision, and priorities are, to a certain degree, also determined by institutions in their wider environment such as education, professional associations, tradition, hypes, etc. For example, a mainland European-educated HR professional will take it for granted that we have workers' participation and voice, very often by means of a works council, whereas someone trained in the USA and starting to work for a European subsidiary of a USA-multinational firm will, in the first instance, be surprised about the degree of influence that is attached to the (formal) role of a works council. As organizations (and thus HRM) are deeply embedded in their wider institutional environment, only analysing the market forces impacting on the organization is not sufficient. The behaviour of organizations is also subject (whether we like it or not) to institutional pressures from all kinds of regulatory bodies (state, European legislation, agreements between social partners, trade unions, etc.), professional bodies, and from general societal expectations (Greenwood & Hinings, 1996). Organizations are not only motivated by efficiency and effectiveness but also by legitimacy (Lewis et al., 2018). After all, the degree to which an organization is perceived to be legitimate by society at large depends on its adherence to values, norms, traditions, etc. In this way, every organization faces two challenges: being efficient and effective based on rationality and being perceived as legitimate based on adherence to norms, values, traditions, and general societal expectations and trends.

2.   FOUNDING FATHERS/MOTHERS/STATUS/ RELEVANCE

Institutional theory covers many domains and has different strands. Here, we focus on institutional theory from a sociological perspective and primarily its relevance for HRM theorizing and practices. As many disciplines and theorists make use of institutional theory and have helped to develop it, it is difficult to identify one founding father or mother. It is more a whole family, the members of which have made important contributions. Just to name a few: Selznick, Meyer and Rowan, Scott, Dimaggio and Powell, Oliver, Zucker, and Greenwood.

Institutional theory has invaded many disciplines such as economics, sociology, history, political sciences, organizational theory, and the field of HRM. It is a very well-established field of academic enquiry, of which the results have been published in top-tier journals such as *Academy of Management Review*, *American Sociological Review*, *Academy of Management Journal*, *Administrative Science Quarterly*, *American Journal of Sociology*, and *Organization Studies*. For those interested in further reading, Lewis et al. (2018) in *Human Resource Management Review* offer an excellent systematic review on the background, meaning, and implications of applying an institutional perspective in the knowledge domain of HRM.

3.   CONTENT OF THE THEORY

Trying to understand why HRM is as it is, requires the awareness that organizations not only react to market pressures or budgetary constraints and facilities (non-profit sector), but that they are also deeply embedded in societal expectations (formed by tradition, habits, laws, etc.) which influence the structuring and behaviour of organizations (Dacin, 1997, p. 48). This influence can be so pervasive that complying with societal expectations takes on an almost for-granted nature. Without thinking, we comply with all kinds of norms, habits, regulations, etc. Related to an HRM practice such as working overtime, this will qualify for being paid extra. At the same time, we see that those kinds of taken for granted norms are subject to change. Many retail chains have stopped paying extra in these circumstances as society at large considers it quite normal that shops are open 24/7. Employees simply accept working during the weekend or at night as part of the game for which no extra payment is expected. This implies that institutional theory makes us aware of the constraints (institutions as a constraining force, limiting strategic choice), but that at the same time institutions are subject to change and that people can respond differently to the pressures being exerted by institutions. They can comply but they can also escape from it by opting for another scenario. This also demonstrates the importance of the interaction between institutions and human agency as a consequence of which institutions – in spite of their enduring nature – can also be subject to change, albeit that this might take some time. By 'human agency' here, we mean the capacity of an actor to act in a given environment.

Constraints

Organizations operating in the same sector or industry are subject to similar institutional mechanisms. For example, in the building sector they all have to comply with the same set of safety regulations. These organizations conform to contextual expectations in order to gain legitimacy and increase their probability of survival (Greenwood & Hinings, 1996). The resulting effect is that these organizations become increasingly more similar. Dimaggio and Powell (1983) call this process isomorphism (literally translated as 'sameness' or 'similar due to a process of convergence'), which they define as a constraining process that forces one unit, one organization in a population to resemble other units that are exposed to the same set of environmental conditions. By 'population' (or 'organizational field') the authors mean a group of organizations ('units') operating in the same sector/industry.[2] Institutional isomorphism is, according to Dimaggio and Powell (1983), being brought about by three mechanisms which impact decision making in organizations, see also Figure 2.1 (Paauwe & Boselie, 2003, p. 61):

- *Coercive mechanisms*, which stem from political influence and the problem of legitimacy. Related to HRM, we can think of the influence of social partners (the trade unions and works councils), labour legislation, and government.
- *Mimetic mechanisms*, which result from standard responses to uncertainty. This mechanism refers to imitations of the strategies and practices of competitors because of uncertainty or fashionable fads in the field of management. Organizations' current interest in abandoning annual performance appraisals (e.g., Buckingham & Goodall, 2015) could be a typical example of a mimetic mechanism in the field of HRM (Paauwe & Farndale, 2017, p. 67). Another example is the hype around people analytics and making use of so-called big data.
- *Normative mechanisms*, which are associated with professionalization. Normative mechanisms refer to the relationship between management policies and the background of employees in terms of educational level, job experience, and professional networks (Powell & DiMaggio, 1991). Professional networks consist of, for example, universities and professional training institutes that develop and reproduce (taken for granted) organizational norms among professional managers and staff specialists in the different functional areas of finance, marketing, accounting, and HRM (Paauwe & Farndale, 2017, p. 67).

In a similar vein, Scott (2008) presents a framework to understand the content of institutions and sources of isomorphism by distinguishing three different pillars:

- *The regulative pillar*: Laws and regulations, inclusive enforcement mechanisms, for example laws and agreement with trade unions on participation and voice.

- *The normative pillar*: Socially held norms and values pertaining to appropriate behaviour, which become internalized through processes of socialization; for example, being in time for an appointment and properly dressed, or sticking to an agreement, even if nothing has been written down.
- *The cultural-cognitive pillar*: Reflecting the cognitive structures and knowledge shared by people in a given sector, region, or country. These constitute the nature of reality and the frames through which meaning is made (Paauwe & Farndale, 2017, p. 72; Scott, 2008). A pillar which mainly influences individual level perception. An example of this are the stereotypes people hold about people in other regions or other countries, etc., for example, a long existing stereotype about the success of British/ Dutch collaboration (think of Shell, Unilever) is that the British people have the imagination and the vision, whereas the Dutch people will make sure that it is being implemented and done.

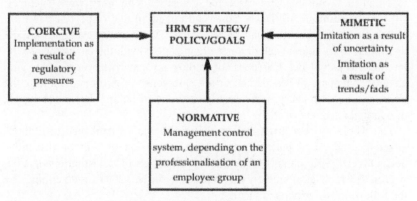

Note: Reprinted from 'Challenging "Strategic HRM" and the relevance of the institutional setting, 2003, by J. Paauwe and P. Boselie, *Human Resource Management Journal*, 13, p. 61 (*https://doi.org/10.1111/j.1748-8583.2003.tb00098.x*). Copyright 2003 by Eclipse Group Ltd.

Figure 2.1   HRM and new institutionalism

4.   CHANGE, AGENCY, AND INSTITUTIONAL ENTREPRENEURSHIP

Until now we have mainly emphasized how institutional mechanisms constrain the choice for organizational structuring and practices. However, institutional theory can also account for change.[3] One can imagine that the normative embeddedness of an organization within its institutional context can also form a major source of organizational resistance to change. In this respect, it is important to focus on the interaction between (institutional) context, intra-organizational dynamics and the role of individuals (actors, human agency) in making choices. Oliver (1991) shows how organizations can respond to institutional processes as they use different strategies (options) to respond to these processes ranging from acquiescence to manipulation. The following scheme (Table 2.1), taken from Oliver (1991, p.152), gives an overview of the range of strategies/options.

A limitation of this overview is that the responses are formulated either in a con-forming way ('acquiesce' and 'compromise') or in a negative way ('avoid', 'defy', 'manipulate'). One can also imagine more positive and constructive options such as 'lead', 'initiate', or 'develop'. Examples in this respect are companies who settle for a labour agreement with their works council instead of with the trade unions in their sector. Or a company like Randstad, of which the founder/owner Frits Goldschmeding, back in the 1960s/1970s, managed to create a favourable and respected image of temporary work agencies, while in that time it still had a rather bad image. In that respect he can truly be labelled as an 'institutional' entrepreneur.[4] More recent examples are the disruption of traditional cab drivers' organizations with the emergence of the internet company Uber, who does not employ any cabdriver, yet is able to gain a significant share of the market, or the emergence of Airbnb, disrupting the traditional hotel industry with a totally new way of linking demand to supply of overnight accommodation.

The whole process of change implies that certain established institution-alized practices and patterns are subject to erosion or will be discontin-ued. Oliver (1992, p. 564) labels this as a process of deinstitutionalization. A process which, as eloquently summarized by Jaffee (2001), is determined by the following two groups of factors:

- *Intra-organizational determinants*: 'Pressures may arise within the organ-ization as new members are recruited, performance declines, and power alignments shift, goals are more clearly defined, or the organizational structure is transformed owing to diversification or mergers. These rather common events can conceivably threaten, or at least call into question, institutionalized patterns of organization and behaviour and stimulate change' (Jaffee, 2001, p. 235; Oliver, 1992, p. 579).
- *External environmental forces*: 'These might include increasing compe-tition or environmental turbulence, changes in government regulations, shifts in public opinion, dramatic events or crises and changes in task environment relationships' (Jaffee, 2001, p. 235; Oliver, 1992, p. 579).

Table 2.1   Strategic responses to institutional processes

Strategies	Tactics	Examples
Acquiesce	Habit	Following invisible, taken-for-granted norms
	Imitate	Mimicking institutional models
	Comply	Obeying rules and accepting norms
Compromise	Balance	Balancing the expectations of multiple constituents
	Pacify	Placating and accommodating institutional elements
	Bargain	Negotiating with institutional stakeholders
Avoid	Conceal	Disguising non-conformity
	Buffer	Loosening institutional attachments
	Escape	Changing goals, activities, or domains
Defy	Dismiss	Ignoring explicit norms and values
	Challenge	Contesting rules and requirements
	Attack	Assaulting the sources of institutional pressure
Manipulate	Co-opt	Importing influential constituents
	Influence	Shaping values and criteria
	Control	Dominating institutional constituents and process

Note: Reprinted from 'Strategic responses to institutional processes', by C. Oliver, 1991, *Academy of Management Review*, 16(1), p. 152 (https://doi.org/10.5465/amr.1991.4279002). Copyright 1991 by Academy of Management Review.

Institutional Logics

An increasingly popular area of institutional theory that accounts for the role of agency in (institutional) change processes is related to institutional logics (Friedland & Alford, 1991; Thornton et al., 2012). According to Scott et al. (2000), institutional logics can be defined as 'the belief systems and associated practices that predominate in an organizational field' (p. 170). As indicated beforehand, an organizational field refers to a group of organizations operating in the same sector, for example hospitals. These logics determine the suitability of managerial practices, such as HRM practices, in certain contexts and situations (Greenwood et al., 2010). Institutional logics are capable of guiding the attention of organizational decision-makers to specific issues and influence decisions such that they will be coherent with the logic (Ocasio, 1997; Van den Broek et al., 2013). Therefore, this perspective accounts for change and agency in organizations due to the presence of institutional logics (Thornton et al., 2012). Often, organizations are confronted with multiple and sometimes even conflicting institutional logics (Pache & Santos, 2010; Thornton & Ocasio, 2008), referred to as institutional complexity.

Frequently occurring and opposing logics are the market logic and the professional logic. The market logic focuses on exchange, transactions, self-interest, making a profit, etc., whereas the professional logic emphasizes expertise, status of the profession, linkages with the professional associations, reputation, etc. (Lewis et al., 2018, p. 327). Box 2.1 presents a case study of the adoption and implementation of an HRM-related innovation process in such an institutionally complex field as healthcare, with two competing institutional logics (market versus professional).

BOX 2.1   COMPETING LOGICS IN A HOSPITAL WARD

Similar to hospitals in other countries, Dutch hospitals are confronted by the challenge of enhancing the quality, while at the same time reducing the cost of care. Several scholars (e.g., Kitchener, 2002; Reay & Hinings, 2009) acknowledge this development by indicating shifts in institutional logics in the healthcare field from a professional logic to a market logic. The traditional professional logic means that factors such as prestige and technical quality of care determine the legitimacy of services (Kitchener, 2002), while the market logic primarily views cost reduction as an important parameter (Reay & Hinings, 2009). Nowadays, both professional and market logics seem to be affecting the healthcare industry, for example, by influencing decision-making and implementation processes around the adoption of HRM-related innovations.

In a longitudinal case study ('Productive Ward: Releasing Time to Care'), insights into the adoption, decision-making and implementation process of an apparently hybrid innovative practice were explored. The case involves a quality improvement program that aimed to empower nursing staff to improve the care processes in their wards, the aims being to release more time for direct patient care ('Releasing Time to Care'), a higher quality of care, more satisfied patients and nurses, and a decreasing amount of waste ('Productive Ward'). This is an interesting innovation to study in the health-care context, because, at first glance, the program seems to combine the two logics with which hospital organizations are confronted. The title of the case suggests its hybrid nature, incorporating both a nursing professional logic ('Releasing Time to Care') and a market logic ('Productive Ward').

Initially, the findings in this case-study demonstrated that key decision makers referred to both types of logic when discussing the program. The labelling and communication of the program throughout the organization seemed to play an important role in this. However, in the end, the findings indicated that although appearing to incorporate both logics, in practice, the main goals were to accomplish those aims that suited the market log-ic rather than both logics simultaneously. In addition, internal presentation and execution of the program as fitting the professional logic of nurses did not deliver intended results, partly because of the suspicion (and right they were!) that was created among nurses due to the double labelling of the program.

Note: Adapted from 'Multiple institutional logics in health care: Productive ward: "Releasing time to care"', by J. Van den Broek, P. Boselie and J. Paauwe, 2003, *Public Management Review,* 16, 1–20 (https://doi/org/10.1080/14719037.2013.770059). Copyright 2013 by Taylor & Francis. Adapted with permission.

5.   EMPIRICAL EVIDENCE AND APPLICATIONS OF INSTITUTIONAL THEORY

Based on the use of institutional theory in different disciplines, the empirical evidence and applications are widespread. Below, we focus on applications in the domain of HRM. Based on a systematic review, Lewis et al. (2018) made an inventory of all the conceptualizations and empirical evidence of institutional theory related to HRM. The systematic overview results in 64 (!) articles, the essence of which can be read in the Lewis et al. (2018) paper. Below we give a few examples just by way of illustration.

*   Collective bargaining in the UK is resilient to change due to its institution-alization as well as its coercive institutional pressures (Beszter et al., 2015).
*   The more institutionalized an industry, the weaker the effect of HRM on performance. This is due to the constraints placed on HRM in highly institutionalized environments. By this we mean an environment – or

sector – with strong labour legislation and powerful trade unions (Boselie et al., 2003).

• Local isomorphic forces (at the national level) push back against the global adoption of HRM practices in MNC subsidiaries (Brewster et al., 2008).

• The institutional environment can hamper the success of high-performance work systems; however, the institutional environments of emerging economies are highly supportive of the implementation of high-performance work systems (Lawler et al., 2011).

• The institutional pressure explains the adoption of 12 out of the 16 so-called best practices as defined by Pfeffer in the Netherlands (Boselie et al., 2001).

• The employment of host country nationals by MNC subsidiaries increases subsidiary legitimacy (Forstenlechner & Mellahi, 2011).

NOTES

1. This chapter is to a large degree based on Paauwe & Farndale (2017), *Strategy, HRM and Performance: A Contextual Approach*, Chapter 4, pp. 65–74.
2. Powell and DiMaggio (1991, pp. 64–65) define the concept of organizational field as 'those organizations that in the aggregate, constitute a recognized area of institutional life: key suppliers, resource and product consumers, regulatory agencies, and other organizations that produce similar services and products'. In short: a sector or industry.
3. In a special issue of the *Academy of Management Journal* (edited by Dacin et al., 2002), a whole range of authors convincingly demonstrate that institutional theory can also account for change.
4. According to Dimaggio (1988), institutional entrepreneurship is the ability of skilled social actors to shape their institutional environment.

REFERENCES

Beszter, P., Ackers, P., & Hislop, D. (2015). Understanding continuity in public sector HRM through neo-institutional theory: Why national collective bargaining has survived in English local government. *Human Resource Management Journal*, 25(3), 364–381. https//doi.org/10.1111/1748-8583.12051.

Boselie, P., Paauwe, J., & Jansen, P. (2001). Human resource management and performance: Lessons from the Netherlands. *International Journal of Human Resource Management*,12(7), 1107–1125. https://doi.org/10.1080/09585190110068331.

Boselie, P., Paauwe, J., & Richardson, R. (2003). Human resource management, institutionalization and organizational performance: A comparison of hospitals, hotels and local government. *The International Journal of Human Resource Management*, 14(8), 1407–1429. https://doi.org/10.1080/0958519032000145828.

Brewster, C., Wood, G., & Brookes, M. (2008). Similarity, isomorphism or duality? Recent survey evidence on the human resource management policies of multi-national corporations. *British Journal of Management*, 19(4), 320–342. https:// doi .org/ 10 .1111/j.1467-8551.2007.00546.x.

Buckingham, M., & Goodall, A. (2015). Reinventing performance management. *Harvard Business Review*, 93(4), 40–50.

Dacin, M. T. (1997). Isomorphism in context: The power and prescription of institutional norms. *Academy of Management Journal*, 40(1), 46–81. https:// doi .org/ 10 .5465/257020.

Dacin, M. T., Goodstein, J., & Scott, W. R. (2002). Institutional theory and institutional change: Introduction to the special research forum. *Academy of Management Journal*, 45(1), 45–56. https://doi.org/10.5465/amj.2002.6283388.

Dimaggio, P. (1988). Interest and agency in institutional theory. In L. G. Zucker (Ed.), *Research on Institutional Patterns: Environment and Culture*. Ballinger Publishing Co.

DiMaggio, P. J., & Powell, W. W. (1983). The iron cage revisited: Institutional isomorphism and collective rationality in organizational fields. *American Sociological Review*, 48(2), 147–160. https://doi.org/10.2307/2095101.

Forstenlechner, I., & Mellahi, K. (2011). Gaining legitimacy through hiring local workforce at a premium: The case of MNEs in the United Arab Emirates. *Journal of World Business*, 46(4), 455–461. https://doi.org/10.1016/j.jwb.2010.10.006.

Friedland, R., & Alford, R. R. (1991). Bringing society back in: Symbols, practices, and institutional contradictions. In W. W. Powell and P. J. DiMaggio (eds), *The New Institutionalism in Organizational Analysis* (pp. 232–263). Chicago: University of Chicago Press.

Greenwood, R., & Hinings, C. R. (1996). Understanding radical organizational change: Bringing together the old and the new institutionalism. *Academy of Management Review*, 21(4), 1022–1054. https://doi.org/10.5465/amr.1996.9704071862.

Greenwood, R., Díaz, A. M., Li, S. X., & Lorente, J. C. (2010). The multiplicity of institutional logics and the heterogeneity of organizational responses. *Organization Science*, 21(2), 521–539. https://doi.org/10.1287/orsc.1090.0453.

Jaffee, D. (2001). *Organization Theory: Tension and Change*. New York: McGraw-Hill.

Kitchener, M. (2002). Mobilizing the logic of managerialism in professional fields: The case of academic health centre mergers. *Organization Studies*, 23(3), 391–420. https://doi.org/10.1177/0170840602233004.

Lammers, C. J., Mijs, A. A., & van Noort, W. J. (2000). *Organisaties vergelijkende wijs: Ontwikkeling en relevantie van het sociologisch denken over organisaties*. Utrecht: Het Spectrum.

Lawler, J. J., Chen, S. J., Wu, P. C., Bae, J., & Bai, B. (2011). High-performance work systems in foreign subsidiaries of American multinationals: An institutional model. *Journal of International Business Studies*, 42(2), 202–220. https://doi.org/10.1057/jibs.2010.42.

Lewis, A. C., Cardy, R. L., & Huang, L. S. R. (2018). Institutional theory and HRM: A new look. *Human Resource Management Review*, 29(3), 316–335. https://doi.org/10.1016/j.hrmr.2018.07.006.

Ocasio, W. (1997). Toward an attention-based view of the firm. *Strategic Management Journal*, 18(S1), 187–206. https://doi.org/10.1002/(SICI)1097-0266(199707)18:1+%3C187::AID-SMJ936%3E3.0.CO;2-K.

Oliver, C. (1991). Strategic responses to institutional processes. *Academy of Management Review*, 16(1), 145–179. https://doi.org/10.5465/amr.1991.4279002.

Oliver, C. (1992). The antecedents of deinstitutionalization. *Organization Studies*, 13(4), 563–588. https://doi.org/10.1177/017084069201300403.

Pache, A. C., & Santos, F. (2010). When worlds collide: The internal dynamics of organizational responses to conflicting institutional demands. *Academy of Management Review*, 35(3), 455–476. https://doi.org/10.5465/amr.35.3.zok455.

Paauwe, J., & Boselie, P. (2003). Challenging 'strategic HRM' and the relevance of the institutional setting. *Human Resource Management Journal*, 13(3), 56–70. https://doi.org/10.1111/j.1748-8583.2003.tb00098.x.

Paauwe, J., & Farndale, E. (2017). Strategy, HRM and Performance: A Contextual Approach (second ed.). Oxford: Oxford University Press.

Powell, W. W., & DiMaggio, P. J. (1991). *The New Institutionalism in Organizational Analysis*. Chicago: University of Chicago Press.

Reay, T., & Hinings, C. R. (2009). Managing the rivalry of competing institutional logics. *Organization Studies*, 30(6), 629–652. https://doi.org/10.1177/0170840609104803.

Scott, W. R. (2008). *Institutions and Organizations*. Thousand Oaks, CA: Sage Publications.

Scott, W. R., Ruef, M., Mendel, M., & Caronna, G. (2000). *Institutional Change and Healthcare Organizations: From Professional Dominance to Managed Care*. Chicago: University of Chicago Press.

Thornton, P. H., & Ocasio, W. (2008). Institutional logics. In R. Greenwood, C. Oliver, K. Sahlin- Andersson and R. Suddaby (eds), *The SAGE Handbook of Organizational Institutionalism* (pp. 99–128). Thousand Oaks, CA: Sage Publications.

Thornton, P. H., Ocasio, W., & Lounsbury, M. (2012). *The Institutional Logics Perspective: A New Approach to Culture, Structure, and Process*. Oxford: Oxford University Press.

Van den Broek, J., Boselie, P., & Paauwe, J. (2013). Multiple institutional logics in health care: Productive ward: Releasing time to care. *Public Management Review*, 16(1), 1–20. https://doi/org/10.1080/14719037.2013.770059.

Zucker, L. (1977). The role of institutionalization in cultural persistence. *American Sociological Review*, 42(5), 726–743. https://doi.org/10.2307/2094862.

3. The contextually-based Human Resource Theory[1]

TRIGGER

Looking at a range of firms and organizations, it is surprising how different their HR policies and systems are. Ranging from very sophisticated (e.g., Shell, IBM) to formalized (e.g., public organizations such as civil service, universities), to very basic (e.g., hospitality industry). The domain of HRM is also highly subject to trends and organizational hypes such as outsourcing, HR shared service centers, HR analytics, etc. One can wonder if these differences and commonalities contribute to an effective HRM – effective in terms of performance and well-being. Popular handbooks offer all kind of recipes and blueprints on how to develop an optimal HRM system, irrespective of the nature of the specific organization or sector in which it is operating. Simply looking at the differences between an accountancy firm and a chicken slaughterhouse demonstrate how different the nature of their work and underlying values are. While in a chicken slaughterhouse it is all about hygiene, safety, and efficiency, the employees of an accountancy firm face values like professionalism, adhering to international accountancy standards, ethical codes, accuracy and last but not least the need for billable hours. These differences in the nature of their work and related values will also impact the design of their HRM system. Working conditions will prevail in the chicken slaughterhouse, whereas in the accountancy firm compliance and professionalism will prevail. This example indicates the need for a customized approach when developing/ designing appropriate HR systems and making sure that we stay away from general recipes and blueprints.

1. DEFINING THE CONCEPT AND HOW IT CAN HELP PRACTITIONERS

An important discussion among both academics and practitioners is the distinction between 'best practices' and 'best fit'. Best practices represent universalistic HR practices, which can be applied, and which will work in every organization irrespective of the sector or country in which the organization is working. Best fit, on the contrary, focuses on the context-dependent nature of HR practices. They need to be adapted according to the specific context in which the organization is operating. Important contextual factors are sector, industry, country, educational level, technical system, organizational culture, size, rate of unionization, legislation, governance structure, etc. The contextually-based human resource theory gives an overview of both external as well as internal contextual factors, helping to map and analyse these and demonstrating how context impacts on the shaping of HR practices. At the same time, the framework also helps to optimize the different forms of fit (strategic fit, internal fit, organizational fit, and institutional fit) in order to achieve simultaneously firm performance, employee well-being, and societal well-being.

2.   FOUNDING FATHERS/MOTHERS/STATUS/ RELEVANCE

The idea about developing a HRM theory, which was more focused on the emergence and shaping of HRM systems instead of its present-day dominant link with performance, dates back to the 1990s, when Paauwe (1994) unfolded his ideas in his inaugural lecture at Erasmus University Rotterdam. By that time, it was also based – next to the contextual dimensions – on the Resource Based View perspective. A theory, which explains a sustained competitive advantage based on internal resources which are valuable, rare, difficult to imitate, and difficult to substitute (see Barney, 1991). Human resources themselves (i.e., employees, workers) would fit these criteria par excellence. Ten years later, a more extensive publication followed, in which all the theoretical building blocks were extensively dealt with in order to be 'assembled' together in the contextually-based human resource theory, in short CBHRT (Paauwe, 2004). Moreover, case studies at organizational and sectoral levels illustrated/explored the newly developed theory. The book draws international attention and was awarded the Dutch HRM Network Award in 2004. In 2017, an updated and fully revised edition of the 2004 book was published together with Farndale as co-author (Paauwe & Farndale, 2017). This updated model for the CBHRT is displayed by Figure 3.1 (Paauwe & Farndale, 2017, p. 103).

3.   CONTENT OF THE THEORETICAL FRAMEWORK

The starting point of the framework are the three mechanisms that impact the shaping of HRM practices. The first, mainly an external contextual factor, are the *competitive mechanisms* arising out of the marketplace, i.e., the way the firm positions itself amidst rivalling firms and the kind of technology it uses. Readers familiar with strategic management will recognize the way of thinking in terms of product/market/technology combinations. With respect to non-profit organizations, we can think of the specific sector the organization is operating in and the kind of demands imposed upon the organization from higher level governing bodies, who will enable the delivery of services and/or products through their budgeting mechanisms. Yet, at the same time, they will also be controlling and monitoring the quality and kind of services delivered (for example, a municipality using taxpayers' money to deliver a range of services of good quality at the lowest possible cost, such as collecting garbage, maintaining the sewage draining system, etc.). The second external factor is the *institutional mechanisms* – the whole set of rules, customs, and traditions of the regulatory setting in which the firm is operating. Think of legislation, the prevailing economic system (liberal or coordinated market economy), sectoral agreements between employers' federations and trade unions, etc. The competitive dimension is embedded in this setting and takes into account the social, cultural, and legal dimensions. Outcomes from a purely competitive, economic way of thinking can be altered due to the need to comply with the institutional setting, in which efficiency or effectiveness are not the dominant criteria, rather criteria such as legitimacy and fairness take priority. Each firm needs external legitimacy, if not it will run the risk of stakeholders withdrawing their resources. For example, customers might stop buying from a company that has been involved in a scandal such as polluting the environment, or for the way in which it treats its employees. Finally, the third factor, relates to the importance of internal contextual factors, such as organizational culture, the kind of systems in use, and the way the organization is structured. All based on a set of interlinked strategic decisions, norms, and values (very often stemming from the founding father or mother) which have taken place in the past (that's why this dimension is called *heritage mechanisms*) and which still, to a certain degree, constrain or facilitate present day and future organizational activities. These three mechanisms will interact and impact each other, which can also imply tensions. From a competitive mechanisms perspective, firms need to differentiate themselves from others to achieve a distinct competitive advantage. At the same time (from the perspective of institutional mechanisms), they need to comply with and conform to all kind of rules, habits, and traditions to be perceived as legitimate. This implies a process of balancing the different contextual forces, which requires a customized approach for every organization to achieve a sustained competitive advantage. An approach which will be carried out by the key decision makers, such as top management, HR director, and works council.

They will be faced with the competitive setting (or budgetary constraints in the case of a non-profit organization), the challenges arising out of the marketplace (or sector), and then having to decide on the kind of organizational capa-

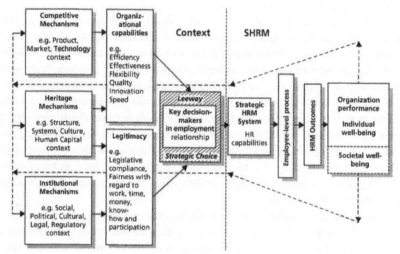

Note: Reprinted from *Strategy, HRM and Performance: A Contextual Approach* (2nd ed.) (p. 103), by J. Paauwe & E. Farndale, 2017, Oxford University Press. Copyright 2017 by Oxford University Press.

Figure 3.1   The contextual strategic HRM model

bilities the organization needs to have to survive (or preferably become 'the best') in the marketplace, in their sector. At the same time, they will analyse the claims for compliance, legitimacy, and fairness based on the institutional setting in which the firm is operating, while at the same time considering the constraints of the firm's heritage. This is not an exercise in which the contextual factors determine the outcome. There is leeway for strategic choice by the key decision makers. Based on the different claims and challenges arising out of the analysis of the three contextual forces, they will start developing their choices for a strategic HRM system, which tries to align and provide answers to both the required capabilities (competitive dimension) and the claims for fairness and legitimacy (institutional dimension), while at the same time taking into account the specific nature of their organization (heritage dimension).

Subsequently, the developed HRM system needs to be implemented with the help of line management and the workers themselves, with the aim of impacting on attitude and behaviour in such a way that positive HR outcomes will be achieved. HR outcomes such as commitment, engagement, well-being, etc. The overall results will be threefold: firm performance, employee well-being, and societal well-being. Not as an 'automatic' result – no, this will be the result of considering – from the very beginning – the three dimensions, analysing them carefully and trying to convert the consequences of such an analysis in a set of required capabilities and justified claims for fairness and legitimacy. Last but not least, the final step: the development of an HRM system which is capable of meeting those demands in a strategic way. Below (see section on Scania) we provide a real-life illustration of how this can become a reality!

4.   THE MORE FITS THE BETTER

Using the contextual strategic HRM model implies a process of joint optimization of both competitive and institutional mechanisms. But there is more to it. Included in its approach and analysis are the four most important fits in HRM. First, *strategic fit*: The alignment between the strategic direction of the firm and its HRM system. Secondly, *environmental or institutional fit*: the alignment between the institutional setting of an organization and its HRM system. Thirdly, *organizational fit*: to what degree is the nature of the designed HRM system in line with organizational systems, technology, heritage, etc. Finally, *internal fit*: the coherence and synergistic effects among the different HRM practices, which together form the HRM system. In Figure 3.2, these different forms of fit are depicted in the framework of the contextual strategic HRM model. As the environment is subject to change, adapting the nature of fit is a continuous process (dynamic fit). For this reason, feedback loops (see the dotted lines) have been included in the model. Outcomes on time interval 1 change the scene in time interval 2 and might require different organizational capabilities and/or changes in claims for fairness and legitimacy. For example, a new competitor or increasing dominance of a new delivery channel (web-based shops) requires the adaptation of the chosen strategy, new organizational capabilities, etc., or changed legislation with respect to the work–life balance necessitates the adaptation of HRM practices in this area.

Empirical Evidence/Usage, Effects, Results

The theory has been used both in research and in practice. As far as research is concerned, the framework proved to fulfill an excellent job in analysing the context of a group of organizations or sector, which enabled a more customized approach to subsequent quantitative research (see, for example, Veld, 2012; Alingh, 2018).

The value of the CBHRT for practitioners is mainly in the use of it as a kind of force field analysis, analysing the different factors impacting the shaping of HRM. The next step is to align the different demands arising out of both the competitive marketplace and the institutional legal setting, doing so in such a way that it –through a customized HRM systems– leads to achieving a sustained competitive advantage, while at the same time safeguarding performance, well-being, and legitimacy. In this way, the theoretical framework has been applied by more than 1,000 participants in all kinds of training programs, representing hundreds of organizations.

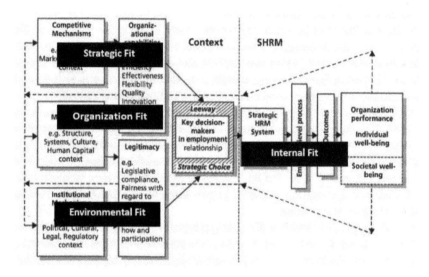

Figure 3.2   Different fits, dynamics and co-evolution

5.   ILLUSTRATION/REFLECTION/REAL LIFE EXAMPLE: SCANIA

Scania is one of the world's leading manufacturers of heavy trucks and buses, established in Sweden, but currently with subsidiaries in more than 100 countries. Here we focus on Scania Production Zwolle in the Netherlands. Since opening in 1964, the workforce in Zwolle has grown to approximately 1,800 employees. In 2013, Scania won the 'HR Proffie Award' (a prize for the best HR policy in the Netherlands).

Scania's objective is to become the best manufacturer of trucks in Europe. To achieve this, Scania emphasizes the following core values: customers first, respect for all employees, and fostering a culture of continuous improvement.

Scania operates in a highly competitive, rapidly changing environment. In order to maintain its competitive advantage, Scania operates based on the 'lean' principles of the Scania Production System (SPS), which implies a continuous focus on improving processes and efficiency. Scania encourages employees to come up with suggestions for improvement to make them more efficient and to be able to provide the highest quality. Once a year, Scania employees complete a survey to measure their work satisfaction and allow them to make suggestions for improvement.

In addition to lean management, Scania needs a large pool of flexible workers to cope with the dynamics in the marketplace, which are closely related to the cyclical nature of the economy. What is particularly impressive in Scania is the alignment between the strategic need for flexibility and lean production and their HRM policies. Although the HRM policies are fully aligned with the principles of lean management, they also meet the demands for legitimacy and fairness. This level of balance between competitive and institutional mechanisms is arguably something that helps to make Scania so successful. Some examples of this are provided below.

Operating in a highly dynamic market requires a flexible workforce along-side those working on a permanent contract. However, these flexible employ-ees also have a need for security, which they can achieve by developing and maintaining appropriate levels of training and skills. Scania offers the pool of flexible workers the same training and development opportunities as are avail-able to the permanent workers. Moreover, the pool of flexible workers is also the main source of recruitment as soon as core employees with a permanent contract leave the company (usually due to retirement). Similarly, flexible workers are offered a permanent contract when the flexible pool exceeds 30% of the total workforce, based on an agreement with the works council. In the previous two years, Scania had offered a permanent contract to approximately 200 workers from the flexible worker pool.

Another development within Scania is the increasing average age of the workforce, among others, due to changed retirement legislation (from 65 to 67). In response, Scania introduced the 'fit for duty' policy. To keep employ-ees 'fit for duty' until they reach the age of 67, Scania invests significantly in behavioral and physical training, aimed at improving the health of all employ-ees. The BRAVO[2] training program, for example, focuses on intensifying physical exercise, quitting smoking, drinking less alcohol, eating healthy food and relaxing. Some 40% of Scania's employees participate in this program. There is a special BRAVO program for older employees that focuses more on changing their lifestyle.

The HRM policies for absenteeism due to illness have also been changed. An employee who is ill has to ask for permission to stay at home, and at the same time a discussion/consultation takes place to see what kind of work-related activities the employee still can do in order to speed up the process of getting back to work. Both the supervisor and employee are responsible for the reinte-gration process. This dual responsibility helped Scania to reduce its absentee-ism rate to less than 4%.

The time it takes to produce one truck, the 'TAKT-time', is a very crucial indicator within an assembly plant. Sometimes employees have difficulties or experience great stress to achieve this TAKT-time. In these cases, employees are able to call an 'Andon'. An 'Andon' is an all-round employee whose job it is to help other employees achieve the TAKT-time. If older or sick employees are frequently unable to keep up with the required TAKT-time, HR management identified this group of workers (80 out of the 1,800 total employees) and created a profile that included all tasks each employee was still able to perform. This profile was then compared to the job description. This comparison showed which job/workplace was best for each employee, and labelled this a 'star-workplace', which means that the company guarantees that the employee can work in that job until retirement. By way of summary, the contextual scan of Scania is depicted in Figure 3.3 (Paauwe & Farndale, 2017, p. 125).

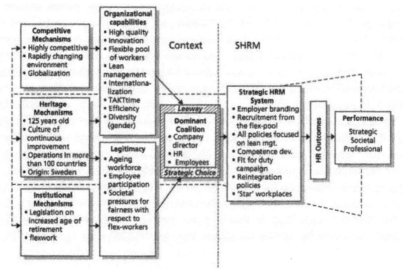

Note: Reprinted from Strategy, HRM and Performance: A Contextual Approach (2nd ed.) (p. 125), by J. Paauwe & E. Farndale, 2017, Oxford University Press. Copyright 2017 by Oxford University Press.

Figure 3.3   The SHRM framework and Scania

NOTES

1.   This chapter is to a large degree based on the book by Paauwe, J. and Farndale, E. (2017). *Strategy, HRM and Performance: A Contextual Approach*, Oxford: OUP, as well as on Farndale, E. and Paauwe, J. (2018). SHRM and context: Why firms want to be as different as legitimately possi-

ble. *Journal of Organizational Effectiveness: People and Performance*, 5(3), 202–210.
2.   The meaning of the acronym 'BRAVO' is Bewegen (moving), Roken (smoking), Alcohol (alcohol), Voeding (food), and Ontspanning (relaxing).

REFERENCES

Alingh, C. W. (2018). *Synergies for Safety: A Theoretical-Empirical Study into Different Safety Management Approaches for Hospital Care*. Erasmus University Rotterdam.
Barney, J. B. (1991). Firm resources and sustained competitive advantage. *Journal of Management*, 17(1), 99–120. https://doi.org/10.1177/014920639101700108.
Farndale, E., & Paauwe, J. (2018). SHRM and context: Why firms want to be as different as legitimately possible. *Journal of Organizational Effectiveness: People and Performance*, 5(3), 202–2010. https://doi.org/10.1108/JOEPP-04-2018-0021.
Paauwe, J. (1994). *Organiseren, een Grensoverschrijdende Passie*. Samsom Bedrijfsinformatie.
Paauwe, J. (2004). *HRM and Performance: Achieving Long Term Viability*. Oxford: Oxford University Press.
Paauwe, J., & Farndale, E. (2017). *Strategy, HRM and Performance: A Contextual Approach* (2nd ed.). Oxford: Oxford University Press.
Veld, M. (2012). *HRM, Strategic Climate and Employee Outcomes in Hospitals*. The Netherlands: lpskamp Drukkers.

4. AMO theory: how to improve abilities, motivation and opportunity to participate

TRIGGER

Human resource management captures many activities such as payroll, administration, keeping records, recruitment, selection, etc. However, what are the activities and HR practices that really add value while at the same time are also appreciated by the workers? Then, we enter the realm of what HRM is all about. How can we improve abilities, how can we strengthen motivation and how can we create an enabling work setting? An enabling work setting and climate where people feel supported, where they can perform, while also experiencing a sense of meaningfulness and a sufficient degree of well-being. If we could discover that kind of HRM perspective and how it manifests itself in practice, then HRM could become crucial in organizations and would be able to make a difference.

1. DEFINING THE CONCEPT AND ITS RELEVANCE FOR PRACTITIONERS

In the last two decades, one of the most applied perspectives on HRM, at least in research, is the so-called AMO framework. AMO is an acronym for Abilities, Motivation and Opportunity. The essence of AMO is as follows: people should be competent, should be motivated and should work in an enabling work setting. Defined in this way, we are able to capture the essence of HRM from a line manager's perspective. Each of the three dimensions of AMO entails a range of different HRM activities, such as recruitment, selection, training, development (A=Ability), rewards, appraisal systems, supervisory behaviour, leadership (M=Motivation) and teamwork, participation, voice, leadership style, job rotation, and job crafting (O=Opportunity to participate). If we group all these activities together in a coherent way, we can call this a High Performance Work System (in short, a HPWS), which is composed of bundles of HRM practices designed to improve firm performance (Paauwe & Farndale,

2017, p. 91) – sometimes also known as high commitment or high involvement work systems. HPWS, grouped in this way, can help to boost performance and improve well-being of the workers. However, it can also create such a committed workforce that the risk of stress and burnout is on the horizon.

2.   FOUNDING FATHER/MOTHER

The AMO framework has become famous through the research of Appelbaum et al. (2000), yet it has its roots much earlier. In this respect, we refer to Blumberg and Pringle (1982), and Cummings and Schwab (1973) as part of a general work performance theory, in which the performance of an individual at work is a function of ability, motivation, and opportunity to perform well. However, applied to the domain of HRM research, many people refer to Eileen Appelbaum (see Appelbaum et al., 2000) as the founding mother. She and her fellow authors have become famous through the much-cited book *Manufacturing Advantage: Why High Performance Work Systems Pay Off*. Doing research in various enterprises and sectors, they were able to demonstrate that HPWS can benefit both the organization and the workers. Surprisingly enough, the phrase 'AMO theory' is not used in their book, but the book does offer a clear representation of the three factors: HRM practices aimed at developing skills and competences, presence of motivation enhancing factors, and opportunity to participate.

3.   CONTENT OF THEORY AND RELATED HRM PRACTICES

Figure 4.1 depicts the framework as developed by Appelbaum and colleagues (2000, p. 27).

In this scheme, we see that the different HRM practices, which relate to the three dimensions of Ability, Motivation, and Opportunity, contribute to effective discretionary effort, which subsequently influences the performance of the firm. What do we mean by discretionary effort? Sometimes people describe it as 'engaged', 'to go the extra mile', or 'to go above and beyond the call of duty'. Actually, it is the difference between what you are required to do based on some kind of job title or job description and what you really want to do in a committed, voluntary, yet effective way, which goes well beyond minimum requirements. People working in this way can really make a difference. A social exchange perspective can best explain the underlying mechanisms, which clarifies why people bother to provide this kind of effort. The three sets of HRM practices, focused on improving your abilities, strengthening your motivation, and giving you the opportunity to participate, imply that you as a worker perceive yourself to be treated well, which you want to reciprocate

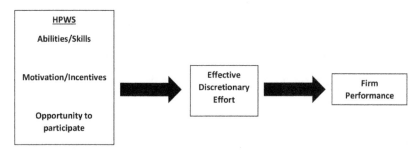

Note: Reprinted from Manufacturing Advantage: Why High Performance Work Systems Pay Off (p. 27), by E. Appelbaum, T. Bailey, P. Berg, and A. Kalleberg, 2000, ILR Press. Copyright 2000 by Cornell University.

Figure 4.1   AMO model

by making – on a voluntarily basis – an extra effort. As far as the different HRM practices are concerned, there is no agreed opinion on what constitutes a HPWS. That is also dependent on the sector in which an organization operates, the educational level, size of the organization, manual labour versus knowledge intensive, etc.

Based on a review study carried out in 2005, Boselie et al. sum up the following HRM practices as most commonly used in the different HPWSs: training and development, contingent pay and reward schemes, performance management (including appraisal), and careful recruitment and selection. The four practices reflect the core of strategic HRM by recruiting strong performers, making sure to provide them with the necessary skills so that they can work with confidence in an effective way, monitoring their progress in relationship with the required targets, and subsequently rewarding them well for meeting or exceeding them (Batt, 2002).

4.   EMPIRICAL EVIDENCE/OUTCOMES

The past 25 years have witnessed a huge increase in research aimed at establishing the link between a set of HRM practices and performance. Below we highlight three meta-analyses which summarize and analyse the data of a large number of previously published papers.

Combs et al. (2006) carried out their meta-analysis based on 92 studies (encompassing almost 20,000 organizations) on the HRM–performance relationship. They found that the more HPWS was used, the higher the performance and the lower the staff turnover.[1] Hence their conclusion that: '… HPWPs' impact on organizational performance is not only statistically significant, but managerially relevant' (Combs et al., 2006, p. 518). They also established that HPWPs – as a bundle of related HRM practices – have a stronger effect than individual HRM practices. The effect size among manufacturing firms was almost twice as large as among service firms. They explained that this may be due to the more complex man–machine/technology interfaces in manufacturing that require more training and instruction (Combs et al., 2006, p. 520).[2]

Subramony (2009, p. 746) carried out a meta-analysis focused on three different HRM bundles aimed at testing the value of bundling HRM practices based on their skill, motivation, and empowerment enhancing effects. We recognize here again the 'AMO' theory of Ability, Motivation, and Opportunity, whereby the latter is defined by Subramony (2009) as 'empowerment enhancing'.

Each bundle represents a set of related HRM practices. The ability bundle, aimed at skill enhancing, includes practices such as recruitment, validated tools for selection, job descriptions, and job-based skill training. The motivation enhancing bundle consists, for example, of HRM practices such as performance appraisal, incentive plans (profit sharing, bonus, etc.), pay related to performance, and internal career opportunities. Finally, the empowerment enhancing bundle, entails HRM practices such as job enrichment (skill flexibility, job variety, responsibility), self-managed or autonomous work groups, employee participation in decision-making, and systems for encouraging feedback from employees (Subramony, 2009, p. 746).

In total, 65 empirical studies are included, published from 1995–2008, which link HRM practices and bundles with business outcomes.

Subramony (2009) establishes that the three bundles have significant and positive relationships with outcomes like employee retention, operating performance (e.g. labour productivity, reduction of waste), and financial performance. The research results also confirm the conclusion by Combs et al. (2006) that bundles/systems have a stronger effect than individual HRM practices. In a similar vein, Subramony (2009) also confirms that the studies conducted in manufacturing samples show significantly larger effect sizes than those based on samples from the service sector.

The meta-analysis by Jiang et al. (2012) explores the mechanisms between HRM systems and both 'proximal' outcomes (human capital and motivation) and 'distal' outcomes (turnover, operational performance such as labour productivity, and financial performance). Proximal implies that the outcome measures are proximal/close to the interventions/HRM practices, whereas distal (further away) implies that the outcome measures can also be influenced by other factors. By including human capital and motivation as mediating variables/intermediate outcomes, they are able to reveal more about the underlying mechanisms through which HRM is associated with different organizational outcomes. As with Subramony (2009), Jiang et al. (2012) conceptualize HRM practices in terms of three distinct bundles: skill-enhancing, motivation-enhancing, and opportunity-enhancing. Skill-enhancing implies strengthening human capital, and motivation-enhancing HRM practices imply increasing the motivation of employees. These two sets are selected as '... the most critical mediating factors' (Jiang et al., 2012, p. 1267). By distinguishing different sets of HRM practices, the authors also shed more light on differential outcomes. For example, skill-enhancing practices mainly increase human capital and to a lesser degree have an impact on motivation. This study involves 116 papers and includes more than 30,000 organizations in total.

Jiang et al.'s (2012) findings reveal that all three HRM dimensions have significant and positive effects on human capital and motivation, and as hypothesized, skill-enhancing HRM practices explained the largest percentage of variance in human capital. Motivation-enhancing and opportunity-enhancing HRM practices had a significantly stronger effect on motivation than the skill-enhancing set of HRM practices, as was expected. They also found a mediating effect of operational and employee-level outcomes between HRM practices and financial outcomes. 'In sum, these results support that

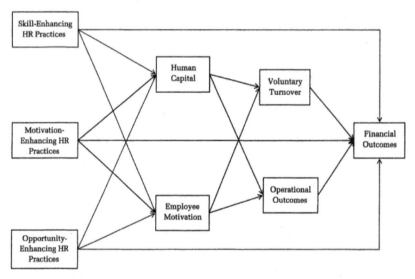

Note: Reprinted from 'How does human resource management influence organizational outcomes? A meta-analytic investigation of mediating mechanisms', by K. Jiang, D. P. Lepak, J. Hu, and J. C. Baer, 2012, Academy of Management Journal, 55, p. 1274 (https://doi.org/10.5465/amj.2011.0088). Copyright 2012 by Academy of Management Journal.

Figure 4.2   Theoretical model of effects of HR dimensions on
*   organizational outcomes*

human capital, employee motivation, voluntary turnover, and operational outcomes partially mediated the relationships between skill-enhancing and motivation-enhancing HR dimensions and financial outcomes and fully mediated the relationship between opportunity-enhancing HR practices and financial outcomes' (Jiang et al., 2012, p. 1274) (see Figure 4.2).

5.   APPLICATION/USAGE

Establishing a high performing organization is the wish of every manager. If we summarize a number of insights not only from academics but also from consultants, we can mention the following insights from a business studies perspective (Paauwe & Farndale, 2017):

- Challenging targets/customer-orientated units: customer first in every aspect of the business and working with targets which require everybody to try as hard as one can.
- Decentralization/delegation of decision making; provided people are capable enough to take on this kind of responsibility.
- Work by semi-autonomous task groups/teamwork.
- Performance management at individual level, linked to overall performance indicators. This will help to see the link between individual contribution and unit or firm performance.
- Business process reengineering: making sure that all processes have a connection and contribute to value adding activities aimed at the final customer. If not, these activities should be removed, unless they are required by law, compliance, safety, etc.
- Benchmarking performance in order to learn, improve, and increase shareholder value.
- Creating and stimulating learning and development at all organizational levels: whether the company is doing well or facing difficulties, continuing investments in learning and development is crucial.
- Information and communication: switch from top-down communication to information flowing in all directions. In this way, one can stimulate 'ownership' at all levels in the organization.

The next step is to translate these broad business and organizational principles into implications from the HRM perspective. In this respect, Lawler did a great job by studying high performing firms over the course of many years and being especially interested in the 'people' element of high performing organizations.

His research (Lawler, 2005; Paauwe & Farndale, 2017) resulted, among others, in the following common elements:

- Create a value proposition that defines the workplace: by this, we mean that the way in which an individual adds values to the organization can be understood by the worker, including the way in which his/her contribution is part of the overall value chain.
- Hire people that fit the values, core competences and strategic goals of the organization: this is all about the affinity (preferably said passion) of the worker with the primary processes of an organization.
- Continuously train employees to do their jobs and offer them opportunities to grow and develop.
- Design work that is meaningful and provides feedback, responsibility, and autonomy.
- Have a mission, strategies, goals, and values that employees understand, support, and believe in.
- Have reward systems that reinforce core values and strategy: it is important the reward systems reflect what is really valued (in terms of attitude and behaviour) by the organization.
- Hire and develop leaders who create commitment, trust, and a motivational work environment.

One can imagine that overlooking all these elements for establishing a high-performance work system will form a challenging agenda for both the line and the HR manager, preferably working together in order to make this happen. Being aware of the 'system' nature is crucial. It will not work if we only focus on a few elements. The different parts form a coherent approach (in German: 'Gestalt') with synergistic effects on performance.

The third step it to consider what kind of specific HRM practices will enable a high performance work system. Based upon an inventory of the main empirical research projects in the area of AMO theory and HPWS as carried out by Bos-Nehles (2019) we can give the following overview of HRM practices:

- *Abilities*: Selection, recruitment, training, development, performance evaluation.
- *Motivation*: performance management, appraisal interviews, rewards, promotion and career development, job security, work-life balance, recognition.
- *Opportunity*: the way the work is structured, task design, participation, empowerment, involvement in decision making, teamwork, grievance procedures, sharing of information.

6. A FEW CRITICAL NOTES

Individual Level Versus System Level

Originally, the AMO theory was developed to explain the performance of an individual based on ability, motivation, and opportunity. In HRM research, this has been lifted up to the organizational and system level (the HPWS), whereby the focus shifted from the individual to HRM practices as outlined above. Yet, we have to be aware that a change in performance (be it at the individual, team, or firm level) can only take place through the attitude and behaviour of individuals (Kellner et al., 2019). This also implies that performance is not only dependent upon AMO-related HRM practices but will also depend upon individual characteristics. Kellner et al. (2019) mention in this respect characteristics such as age, health, intelligence, knowledge, skills, energy levels, etc. (all related to ability) and characteristics such as job satisfaction, attitude, engagement, self-image, etc. (all related to motivation).

Multiple Roads to Rome

In this chapter, we have focused on the importance of HRM practices, influencing ability, motivation, and opportunity. However, there are more ways to improve performance (Peccei et al., 2013). Think of the importance of well-being, organizational climate, the way of managing and coordinating employee relations, leadership style, etc. HRM practices are not the silver bullet. Whether they indeed impact on performance in a positive way, depends upon their embeddedness in the organizational setting, among which organizational culture, climate, trust, and leadership are crucial (Paauwe & Farndale, 2017).

Interactive and Iterative Relationships

Based on the distinction between ability and motivational characteristics at the individual level and HRM practices intended to further ability and motivation at the organizational level, we can easily see how all these elements interact with each other in a work setting, which offers opportunities such as working conditions, leadership behaviour, information, feedback, etc. (Kellner et al., 2019). Instead of a rather straight forward framework as originally depicted by Appelbaum et al. (2000) (see Figure 4.1) with a causal link running from AMO-related HRM practices, stimulating discretionary effort to firm performance, reality is much more dynamic. Both in time and space, individual dimensions (ability, motivation) interact with given opportunities in the work setting and HPWS practices at the system/organizational level. In an interactive way, this will influence performance, while at the same time the actual performance will also feedback on ability and performance and might lead to revision of HPWS practices. People learn while performing, improve their ability, get more motivated, see and use opportunities in a different way, etc.

By way of summary, Figure 4.3 (Kellner et al., 2019) depicts once more the AMO framework, but in a more dynamic and interactive way, while outlining all the relevant factors as discussed above.

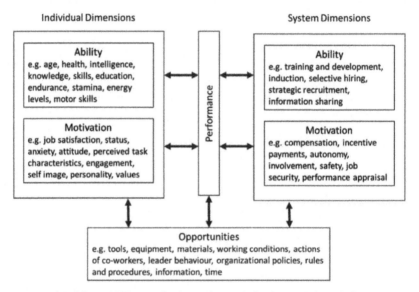

Note: Reprinted from 'Ability, motivation and opportunity theory: A formula for employee performance?', by A. Kellner, K. Cafferkey, and K. Townsend. In Theories of Human Resource Management and Employment Relations (p. 320), by K. Townsend, K. Cafferkey, A. McDermott, and T. Dundon (eds), 2019, Edward Elgar Publishing. Copyright 2019 by K. Townsend, K. Cafferkey, A. McDermott, and T. Dundon.

Figure 4.3   A dynamic model of AMO for HRM

NOTES

1.   More specifically, Combs et al. (2006) found out that an an increase of one standard deviation in the use of HPWPs is associated with a 4.6% increase in return on assets, and with a 4.4% decrease in turnover.

2.   Another reason, according to Combs et al. (2006, p. 520) for the fact that HPWPs affect manufacturers more is: '... that whereas the full range of productive outcomes is largely under the control of manufacturers and thus potentially influenced by HPWPs, production outcomes among services are heavily influenced by customers' ability and willingness to participate (Bowen, 1986) ... Customers therefore limit the range of possible productive outcomes under the influence of HPWPs' (Combs et al., 2006, p. 520).

REFERENCES

Appelbaum, E., Bailey, T., Berg, P., & Kalleberg, A. (2000). *Manufacturing Advantage: Why High Performance Work Systems Pay Off.* Ithaca: ILR Press.

Batt, R. (2002). Managing customer services: Human resource practices, quit rates, and sales growth. *Academy of Management Journal,* 45(3), 587–597. https://doi .org/10.5465/3069383.

Blumberg, M., & Pringle, C. D. (1982). The missing opportunity in organizational research: Some implications for a theory of work performance. *The Academy of Management Review,* 7(4), 560–569. https://doi.org/10.5465/amr.1982.4285240.

Boselie, P., Dietz, G., & Boon, C. (2005). Commonalities and contradictions in HRM and performance research. *Human Resource Management Journal,* 15(3), 67–94. https://doi.org/10.1111/j.1748-8583.2005.tb00154.x.

Bos-Nehles, A. (2019). AMO theory. In W. de Lange, P. De Prins, & B. van der Heijden (eds), *Canon van HRM: 50 theorieën over een vakgebied in ontwikkeling* (pp. 721–736). Vakmedianet.

Bowen, D. E. (1986). Managing customers as human resources in service organiza-tions. *Human Resource Management,* 25(3), 372–384. https://doi.org/10.1002/ hrm.3930250304.

Combs, J., Liu, Y., Hall, A., & Ketchen, D. (2006). How much do high-performance work practices matter? A meta-analysis of their effects on organizational perfor-mance. *Personnel Psychology,* 59(3), 501–528. https://doi.org/10.1111/j.1744 -6570.2006.00045.x.

Cummings, L. L., & Schwab, D. P. (1973). *Performance in Organizations: Determinants & Appraisal.* Scott, Foresman.

Jiang, K., Lepak, D. P., Hu, J., & Baer, J. C. (2012). How does human resource management influence organizational outcomes? A meta-analytic investigation of mediating mechanisms. *Academy of Management Journal,* 55(6), 1264–1294. https://doi.org/10.5465/amj.2011.0088.

Kellner, A., Cafferkey, K., & Townsend, K. (2019). Ability, Motivation and Opportunity theory: A formula for employee performance? In K. Townsend, K. Cafferkey, A. McDermott, & T. Dundon (eds), *Theories of Human Resource Management and Employment Relations* (pp. 311–323). Camberley: Edward Elgar Publishing.

Lawler, E. (2005). Creating high performance organisations. *Asia Pacific Journal of Human Resources,* 43(1), 10–17. https://doi.org/10.1177%2F1038411105050304.

Paauwe, J., & Farndale, E. (2017). *Strategy, HRM, and Performance: A Contextual Approach.* Oxford: Oxford University Press.

Peccei, R., Van de Voorde, K., & Van Veldhoven, M. (2013). HRM, well-being and performance: A theoretical and empirical review. In J. Paauwe, D. Guest, & P.

Wright (eds), *HRM and Performance: Achievements and Challenges* (pp. 15–46). New York: John Wiley & Sons.

Subramony, M. (2009). A meta-analytic investigation of the relationship between HRM bundles and firm performance. *Human Resource Management*, 48(5), 745–768. http://dx.doi.org/10.1002/hrm.20315.

5.   Goal setting theory and feedback[1]

TRIGGER: *THE MAGIC POWER OF GOALS*

Once we become very determined/focused on reaching a certain goal, one often experiences that the resources needed to achieve that goal seem to pop up, as if they materialize out of the blue. Is that really the case or is it simply that having a focus helps us to become more aware of the available resources? Or, do we become more creative in discerning and even creating enabling conditions? A text on a painting (hanging next to my desk) might reveal the secret: 'There is no wind for him/her who has no harbor to sail to'.

1.   DEFINING THE CONCEPT

Goal setting theory (Locke, 1968; Locke & Latham, 1984, 1990, 2002) is a *process* theory about the effectiveness of setting goals and giving feedback in order to stimulate performance. It is based on Ryan's (1970) premise that conscious goals affect action (Locke & Latham, 2002, p. 705). Nowadays, this might seem self-evident, yet by the time of developing their ideas, the so-called *content* theories, such as Maslow's (1943) Need pyramid, Herzberg's (1966) Two factor theory, and McClelland's (1961) Need theory, dominated the scene. The following characteristics of the process of goal setting are important in order to stimulate motivation and subsequent performance. These are:

- Setting specific goals;
  - Which preferably imply a challenge (NB relationship with competence and task complexity);
- Making sure that people are committed to their goals (role of participation, voice); and
- Providing feedback that reveals progress in relation to the stated goal.

2.   FOUNDING FATHERS/MOTHERS

The origin of the goal setting theory dates back to the 1960s and was built and extended over the course of many decades of empirical research by Locke and

Latham. Edwin A. Locke (1938) is now a retired professor of Motivation and Leadership at the Robert H. Smith School of Business at the University in Maryland[2] (USA). The Association for Psychological Science states the following about Locke: 'Locke is the most published organizational psychologist in the history of the field. His pioneering research has advanced and enriched our understanding of work motivation and job satisfaction. The theory that is synonymous with his name – goal setting theory – is perhaps the most widely respected theory in industrial-organizational psychology'. 'A recent survey found that Locke's goal setting theory (developed with G. Latham) was ranked #1 in importance among 73 management theories' (Locke, 2020, introduction section, para. 3).

Gary P. Latham (1949) is a professor of Organizational Behaviour at the Rotman School of Management, University of Toronto (Canada), with cross appointment in the Graduate Faculty in the Centre for Industrial Relations, the Department of Psychology and the Faculty of Nursing. Just like Locke, Latham enjoys an excellent reputation. He has been a former president among others of the Canadian Psychological Association and of the Society for Industrial-Organizational Psychology (SIOP). He is the only recipient of two awards: Distinguished Contributions to Science and ... to Practice from SIOP.

Two landmark books on goal setting theory, jointly written by Locke and Latham are:

- *Goal Setting: A Motivational Technique That Works* (1984);
- *A Theory of Goal Setting and Task Performance* (1990).

Next to these two books, we have made extensive use of their 2002 paper called 'Building a practically useful theory of goal setting and task motivation: A 35-year odyssey', as published in the *American Psychologist* (2002). In this paper, they reflect on their theory development over the course of four decades, including reference to empirical evidence in favour of, or opposing, their theory.

3.   CONTENT OF THEORY/EMPIRICAL EVIDENCE

Locke and Latham formulated their theory in an inductive way based on empirical research. For this reason, we present the different foci of their theory in relation to empirical findings.

- The importance of goal specificity: Locke and Latham (2002, p. 706) contrasted the effect of specific, difficult goals with the general remark of 'do your best'. They found out that specific, difficult goals consistently led to higher performance than urging people to do their best. Effect sizes in meta-analyses range from .42 to .80, which is quite substantial (Locke &

Latham, 1990). The explanation is, according to Locke and Latham that 'do your best goals' have no external reference, so can be interpreted as one likes, leading to a whole range of acceptable performance levels (Locke & Latham, 2002, p. 706), whereas in the case of specific goals, variability is reduced because of reducing the ambiguity about what is to be achieved.

* The importance of self-efficacy: Bandura (1986, 1997) defines this concept as one's belief in one's ability to succeed in specific situations or to accomplish a task. Locke and Latham (2002) define it shortly as task-specific confidence. Locke and Latham (2002, p. 706) indicate that self-efficacy in goal setting theory is quite important to consider. When people are allowed to set their own goals, people scoring higher on self-efficacy set themselves higher goals than people with a lower score on self-efficacy. Higher scoring people are also more committed to assigned goals; finding and using better task strategies in order to reach their goals and reacting more positively to negative feedback (Locke & Latham, 1990; Seijts & Latham, 2001).

* Goal mechanisms: according to Locke and Latham (2002, pp. 706–707), goals impact on performance by means of the following four mechanisms: (1) goals give *direction*, they focus attention and effort towards activities which are relevant for goal achievement; (2) goals *energize*, higher challenging goals generate more energy, more effort than lower, less challenging goals; (3) goals impact *persistence*, if people have the opportunity to control themselves and the time they spend on a task, hard/difficult goals will prolong effort. In this respect, Locke and Latham (2002, p. 707) refer to a trade-off once faced with a difficult goal: '... it is possible to work faster and more intensely for a short period or to work more slowly and less intensely for a long period. Tight deadlines lead to a more rapid work pace than loose deadlines in the laboratory as well as in the field' (Latham & Locke, 1975). Finally, the fourth mechanism: (4) *arousal*, goals impact action in an indirect way by leading to arousal, discovery, creativity, and/ or the use of knowledge relevant for the task.

4. MODERATORS

Next to the way in which goals (and their underlying mechanisms as indicated above) affect directly on performance, the following factors (moderators) also impact on the *relationship* between goals and performance:

* *Goal commitment*: the more committed people are to their goals, the stronger the relationship between goals and performance. Commitment is especially important when goals are perceived as being difficult (Klein

et al., 1999). Factors facilitating commitment to goals are importance, participation, self-efficacy, and feedback (Locke & Latham, 2002, p. 707).

- *Importance*: convincing people that goals are *important* can be done by making a public statement about it or by managers who support the stated goals and develop and express an inspiring vision about it.
- *Participation* is also important for commitment, although the empirical evidence about the difference between participatively set goals and assigned goals, according to Locke and Latham (2002, p. 708) is mixed. However, there is a significant difference between assigned goals, being brief and concise without any explanation, and goals which have been set in a participative way. The latter score significantly higher on performance (Locke & Latham, 2002, p. 708). Next to the motivational effect of participation, Locke et al. (1997) found out that participation mainly has a more cognitive impact in that it stimulates information exchange, which is important for developing task strategies in order to achieve goal attainment.
- *Self-efficacy* enhances goal commitment. Managers can play an important role in this respect by providing adequate training to increase mastery; by referring to role models or acting as a role model themselves, and/or by communicating to the person in charge that one has confidence that he or she can attain the goal (Locke & Latham, 2002, p. 708).
- *Feedback*: the whole process of setting goals and goal attainment becomes more effective when people receive feedback on their progress towards the stated goals.

Another important factor is the degree of *task complexity*, for which the outcomes of empirical research are not unanimous. Sometimes, when complex tasks are at stake, it works better to formulate *learning* goals instead of performance goals. For example, Winters and Latham (1996) found out that '... When a specific difficult learning goal rather than a performance goal was set, high goals led to significantly higher performance on a complex task than did the general goal of urging people to do their best' (Locke & Latham, 2002, p. 709). In the case of having to do new, complex tasks in order to achieve goal attainment, it can also be helpful to formulate proximal, intermediate goals, provided that the decomposition of an overall distal goal into several proximal goals is being done in the right way (Locke & Latham, 2002, p. 709).

5.   USAGE IN PRACTICE

A whole range of studies, for which we refer to the overview by Locke and Latham (2002), provide evidence that it is helpful to work with specific, difficult, and/or challenging goals. They increase productivity and contribute to organizational profitability (Locke & Latham, 2002, p. 711) and thus adding value. Once more, in this respect, specific goals work better (in terms of higher performance) than the simple statement of '... do your best'. One can imagine that these findings are also important for the way in which performance management and performance appraisal are being conducted. Nowadays we see a trend in companies to move away from the once-a-year ritual of end-of-year conversations/appraisal interviews. Instead, a number of organizations are experimenting with frequent intervals of feedback and appraisal, for example directly after finishing a project or assignment. One can imagine that setting specific goals is important in this respect. These goals will not only increase performance but also satisfaction. For an overview of all the factors we have discussed so far, see the 'high performance work cycle' as developed by Locke and Latham (2002, p. 714) (see Figure 5.1).

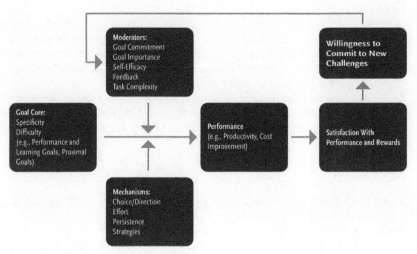

Note: Reprinted from 'Building a practically useful theory of goal-setting and task motivation', by E. A. Locke and G. P. Latham, 2002, American Psychological Association, 57(9), p. 714 (https://doi.org/10.1037/0003-066X.57.9.705). Copyright 2022 by American Psychological Association.

Figure 5.1   *Essential elements of goal-setting theory and the high-performance cycle*

The goal setting theory has been tested extensively across decades of research involving different tasks and in various countries, both in laboratories and simulation settings as well as in real life field settings. Overall, this has led to the consistent outcome that specific, difficult goals increase performance (Locke & Latham, 2002, p. 714). The dependent variables (i.e., performance) have included indicators such as quantity, quality, time spent, costs and measures of job behaviour, etc. Locke and Latham (2002, p. 714) further indicate that the theory is not only able to generate performance effects at the individual level, but is also applicable to groups (O'Leary-Kelly et al., 1994), organizational units (Rogers & Hunter, 1991) and entire organizations (Baum, Locke, & Smith, 2001). With reference to Lee and Early (1992), Miner (1984), and Pinder (1998), the authors themselves conclude that goal setting theory is among the most valid and practical theories of employee motivation (Locke & Latham, 2002, p. 714). So we can really speak of a tested theory in the true meaning of the word 'tested' on the basis of extensive empirical data. The spread across tasks, countries, and research settings (in both experiments as well as field work) adds to its generalizability.

NOTES

1. Every effort has been made to clear copyright for any figures that were originally published elsewhere. Notifications of any additions should be made to the author and the publisher of the material and amendment will be made to the ebook at the earliest opportunity.
2. I recall visiting University of Maryland back in 1994 and was so surprised to find out that behind almost every door of the department there was a famous professor residing – among which was Ed Locke. We shook hands and had a brief chat.

REFERENCES

Bandura, A. (1986). *Social Foundations of Thought and Action: A Social-cognitive Theory*. Hoboken, NJ: Prentice Hall.

Bandura, A. (1997). *Self-efficacy: The Exercise of Control*. Freeman.

Baum, J. R., Locke, E. A., & Smith, K. G. (2001). A multi-dimensional model of venture growth. *Academy of Management Journal*, 44(2), 292–303. https://doi.org/10.5465/3069456.

Herzberg, F. (1966). *Work and the Nature of Man*. New York: World Publishing.

Klein, H., Wesson, M., Hollenbeck, J., & Alge, B. (1999). Goal commitment and the goal-setting process: Conceptual clarification and empirical synthesis. *Journal of Applied Psychology*, 84(6), 885–896. https://doi.org/10.1037/0021-9010.84.6.885.

Latham, G. P., & Locke, E. A. (1975). Increasing productivity with decreasing time limits: A field replication of Parkinson's law. *Journal of Applied Psychology*, 60(4), 524–526. https://psycnet.apa.org/doi/10.1037/h0076916.

Lee, C., & Earley, P. C. (1992). Comparative peer evaluations of organizational behavior theories. *Organization Development Journal*, 10(4), 37–42.

Locke, E. A. (1968). Towards a theory of task motivation and incentives. *Organizational Behavior and Human Performance*, 3(2), 157–189. https://doi.org/10.1016/0030-5073(68)90004-4.

Locke, E. A. (2020). *Introduction*. https://edwinlocke.com/.

Locke, E. A., & Latham, G. P. (1984). *Goal Setting: A Motivational Technique That Works*. Hoboken, NJ: Prentice Hall.

Locke, E. A., & Latham, G. P. (1990). *A Theory of Goal Setting and Task Performance*. Hoboken, NJ: Prentice Hall.

Locke, E. A., & Latham, G. P. (2002). Building a practically useful theory of goal setting and task motivation: A 35-year odyssey. *American Psychologist*, 57(9), 705–717. https://doi.org/10.1037/0003-066X.57.9.705.

Locke, E. A., Alavi, M., & Wagner, J. (1997). Participation in decision-making: An information exchange perspective. In G. R. Ferris (ed.), *Research in Personnel and Human Resources Management*, 15, 293–331. JAI Press.

Maslow, A. H. (1943). A theory of human motivation. *Psychological Review*, 50(4), 370–396. https://doi.org/10.1037/11305-004.

McClelland, D. C. (1961). *The Achieving Society*. New York: Van Nostrand.

Miner, J. B. (1984). The validity and usefulness of theories in emerging organizational science. *Academy of Management Review*, 9(2), 296–306. https://doi.org/10.5465/amr.1984.4277659.

O-Leary-Kelly, A. M., Martocchio, J. J., & Frink, D. D. (1994). A review of the influence of group goals on group performance. *Academy of Management Journal*, 37(5), 1285–1301. https://doi.org/10.5465/256673

Pinder, C. (1998). *Work Motivation in Organizational Behavior*. Hoboken, NJ: Prentice Hall.

Rogers, R., & Hunter, J. E. (1991). Impact of management by objectives on organizational productivity. *Journal of Applied Psychology*, 76(2), 322–336. https://doi.org/10.1037/0021-9010.76.2.322

Ryan, T. A. (1970). *Intentional Behavior*. Ronald Press.

Seijts, G. H., & Latham, G. P. (2001). The effect of learning, outcome, and proximal goals on a moderately complex task. *Journal of Organizational Behavior*, 22(3), 291–302. https://doi.org/10.1002/job.70.

Winters, D., & Latham, G. P. (1996). The effect of learning verses outcome goals on a simple versus a complex task. *Group and Organizational Management*, 21(2), 236–250. https://doi.org/10.1177/1059601196212007.

6.   Human capital and the differentiated approach to employees

TRIGGER

A Strategic Investment in Human Capital for Achieving Competitive Advantage

As a management trainee, I started to work for a modest multinational company where I was seconded to their division of installation companies, which (about 40 subsidiaries in total) were working on a regional basis involved in either heating or electrical installations. I was mentored by the Head of Training and Development and that worked out quite well. We still meet every year for a dinner in a fine fish restaurant overlooking the sea. I learned a lot from him as we were about to start a new training program for middle managers across the whole of the company. The new program had to do with shifting market trends, which implied a bigger demand for integrated installation projects whereby heating and electrical/electronic applications had to be installed jointly. Not every subsidiary was equipped to do so. Moreover, the teams working either in heating or in electrical engineering were not used to working together, in fact, we could discern a certain degree of animosity. Moreover, there was also a strong difference in culture and ways of working together. We needed to make sure that that the different teams could get along and engage in a successful collaboration for realizing the kind of integrated projects the market was asking for. An analysis revealed the need for more training in soft and collaborative skills. But how could we make such a program attractive for a target group mainly consisting of people with a technical background, who thought that being trained in so-called soft skills was only a waste of time and not worth the effort? We decided to call the program Project Management. After all, that's what they were used to: managing projects. We also decided to form mixed training groups (so both heating and electrical installation were represented) and we invested heavily in a preceding training program called 'Train the trainers'. So, we trained the level of managers and staff members, to whom these middle managers were reporting, as trainers of the program on Project Management. These people had the credibility, the status, and were convinced – on the basis of their strategic position – that the future was in working together across the (until that moment) still separately working disciplines. The real content – apart from providing some hard tools for project management – was still very much focused on developing soft and collaboration skills, without promoting that too much in advance. So, we were not facing a lot of resistance for enrolling into the program and once in it, they enjoined the experience, including the so-called soft skills. The program itself became a big success. It was expensive – also due to the missed hours – but the return on investment in the long run was huge as it benefitted a more integrative way of working, and more understanding and respect of each middle manager for his/her colleague working in the other discipline.

1. DEFINING THE CONCEPT AND ITS RELEVANCE FOR PRACTITIONERS

Human capital (HC) theory is a discipline with a long-standing tradition, having its roots within the domain of (labour) economics. An early-stage definition by Schultz (1961, p. 140) describes HC as consisting of the 'knowledge, skills and abilities of the people employed in an organization'. Becker (1993, p. 3) revised his own definition dating back to the 1960s with a modernized one in 1993: the knowledge, information, ideas, skills, and health of individuals. Initially, HC theory focused on explaining economic growth, income inequality and the return on investment of education, training, on the job learning, etc. More recent developments focus on so-called strategic human capital resources, both at the individual and the unit or organizational levels, and how these can contribute to performance and competitive advantage. Both the disciplines of strategic management and strategic human resource management contribute nowadays to the theoretical development of strategic human capital. For practitioners, the theory is relevant for issues like; does investment in training pay off or will it only stimulate turnover? Does strengthening human capital add to the performance of the firm and/or competitive advantage? Do I need to invest in all employees or only in those that contribute disproportionally to performance variability?

2. FOUNDING FATHERS/MOTHERS

The two most pronounced scholars of human capital theory are Gary S. Becker (1964) and Theodore W. Schultz (1961), who both received the Nobel Prize. Next to these two, Jacob Mincer (1958) is also often mentioned. It is a very important stream of theorizing within the economic discipline, but it has gradually extended its impact to other disciplines such as finance, education, strategic management, and HRM. Concepts like resource-based view of the firm, dynamic capabilities, and knowledge-based view can all be linked to Human Capital theory. Its applications go beyond issues of economic growth, income inequality, and whether investing in training and development will pay off.

Nowadays the interaction with other forms of human capital (social, structural, intellectual) is a prominent issue as well as the contribution of human capital to performance and competitive advantage. Present day scholars in this area are Wright, Nyberg, Ployhart, Moliterno, McMahan, and Snell. They have taken the lead in bringing the, until now, separate fields of strategic management (with its focus on the micro foundations of it) and strategic human resource management (with its focus on HRM systems and practices) together, and studying human capital at both the individual and unit/organizational levels, looking at the antecedents and outcomes of Human Capital at different levels of analysis.

3.   CONTENT OF THE THEORY

Human Capital theory is a very broad domain, so summarizing a theory that has evolved over the course of decades and has spread its wings across a variety of disciplines in just a few pages is impossible. Selecting relevant contributions for our readership is the only way out. We do so by focusing – after a general introduction on human capital – on the possibilities for a differentiated approach in HRM, by which we distinguish different groups of employees and workers, in which the organization will invest disproportionately. Of course, this also brings about issues of ethics and well-being, which we will also address. However, first we are going to define and distinguish the concepts of Human Capital, Social Capital, and Structural Capital, which together make up Intellectual Capital.

Using the definitions of Schulz and Becker (see above) as a starting point, a more up to date definition describes HC as the Knowledge, Skills, Abilities and Other characteristics of individuals (KSAOs) used to produce a given outcome (Hitt et al., 2001; Wright & McMahan, 2011). This is typically a definition at the individual level. However, HC is also used at the group, unit, or organizational levels. Then comes the interesting question of how individual HC impacts on and emerges in unit level capabilities and outcomes. Recently, this topic has received a lot of attention under the heading of strategic human capital resources, which according to Ployhart et al. (2014, p. 381) are '… the individual or unit-level (collective) capacities based on individual KSAOs that contribute to competitive advantage'. This emphasis has led academics to a closer relationship between the domains of strategic management and human resource management. This topic is extensively dealt with in Ployhart et al. (2014) as well as in Ployhart and Moliterno (2011), and Boon et al. (2018).

A closely related concept to human capital is *social capital*, which refers '... specifically to the capital embedded within network structures and ties. Social capital helps individuals to connect ideas and knowledge in unforeseen and unusual combinations, which facilitate radical breakthroughs' (McCracken et al., 2017, p. 8). One can imagine that for social capital to flourish, trust is essential.

Finally, *structural capital*, which refers to '...the supportive infrastructure, processes and databases of the organization that enable human and social capital to function' (Ordonez de Pablos et al., 2013, p. 125). So, it encompasses organizational processes, patents, and trademarks, but also the image of the organization, climate, internal structures, information systems, and proprietary databases, or as the authors of the CIPD study on Human Capital put so eloquently: 'The knowledge assets that are left behind, when humans leave work each day' (McCracken et al., 2017, pp. 9–10).

One can imagine that the effectiveness of Human Capital and its capability to add value is highly dependent upon its embeddedness within social and structural capital and the presence of a 'trusting' climate.

4.   HUMAN CAPITAL THEORY AND OUTCOMES

HC theory indicates that employees who invest in training and development will increase their skills, so they will become more productive. In this respect, it is useful to distinguish between general and firm-specific training. According to Becker (1964), firms will be more willing to invest in firm-specific training and are less inclined to invest in general training as in a tight labour market, a firm cannot be sure to get a pay-back on its investment because of the risk of staff turnover. Later on, Estevez-Abe et al. (2001) added industry-specific training to the distinction between general and firm-specific training. Industry-specific training implies boosting productivity of all the employees working in the same industry, which opens up the possibility for sector-wide vocational training facilities and apprenticeships, which are quite common nowadays in many sectors of the economy and of which both the costs and benefits are shared among organizations operating in the same industry. Other relevant outcomes are the ones by Vidal-Salazar et al. (2012), establishing that investment in employee training helps to develop employee capabilities, which facilitate competitive advantage and that employee training also helps to increase commitment. Donate, Pena, and Sanchez de Pablo (2016) found that the combined use of selective staffing, training, and high compensation systems helped to build a firm's level of HC. Finally, the meta-analysis of Subramony (2009) established a positive relationship between a bundle of HR practices, aimed at increasing abilities ('A' as part of the AMO model, see

Chapter 4 of this book) and the level of organizational HC with subsequent links to productivity and financial performance.

5.   APPLICATIONS FOR PRACTITIONERS

The main message of Human Capital theory is that investing in it through education, learning, training, on the job learning, and taking care of health pays off and generates positive outcomes at societal, organizational, and individual levels. But, how about the consequences of differentiating these investments based on distinguishing different categories of employees and/or workers? An issue which will appeal to practitioners working in organizations whose budgets for investing in training and development are limited. Below we highlight several approaches.

Core-Ring Strategies in Order to Cope with Economic Fluctuations

There are several reasons why organizations differentiate between their employees, including different types of labour contract (permanent or temporary workers), or degree of investment in training and development. One prominent reason is, of course, fluctuations in economic cycles. Some industries, such as construction, truck manufacturing, and the automotive industry in general, are very sensitive to these fluctuations. These organizations simply cannot afford to offer everybody a permanent contract. They employ a core group of workers with a permanent contract, in which they also invest (training and development, job rotation, etc.). In addition, they hire a number of peripheral (ring) workers who are employed on temporary contracts in order to cope with the ups and downs of the economic cycle, and for whom investments in training and development are not taken for granted. This model became known as the 'core-ring' strategy of Atkinson (1984).

A Differentiated Approach

Another reason for differentiating the workforce is related to how important employees are for achieving sustainable competitive advantage. Sustainability implies that competitive advantage is based on unique capabilities or resources that cannot be easily imitated by competitors as indicated by the resource-based view of the firm (Barney, 1991). Employees with firm-specific skills are par excellence resources, which cannot easily be imitated/copied by competitors.

In this respect, Lepak and Snell's (1999) framework offers a useful distinction between workers based on two dimensions:

• *Degree of added value of human capital*: Based on the resource-based view of the firm, resources are valuable according to Lepak and Snell (1999, p. 35): 'when they enable a firm to enact strategies that improve efficiency and effectiveness, exploit market opportunities and/or neutralize potential threats'. Considering employees as resources implies that they differ in the degree in which they are able to contribute to the competitive advantage or core competences of the firm. As such, they can be classified as either core or peripheral (as Atkinson (1984) also argued).

• *Degree of uniqueness of human capital*: Again, using resource-based view arguments, the degree of uniqueness or firm specificity will differ per resource, and thus per employee. According to Lepak and Snell (1999), this may be due to unique operational procedures, interdependent arrangements, and team-based production, which will lead to increased social complexity and causal ambiguity, which cannot easily be imitated by competitors. This will also generate tacit knowledge, which again contributes to uniqueness. Moreover, as '... these skills often involve idiosyncratic learning processes, firms are not likely to find these skills in the open labour market' (Lepak & Snell, 1999, p. 35). In the case of uniqueness, the focus will be on developing resources internally, whereas in the case of low or absent uniqueness, this kind of theorizing implies reliance on the external labour market.

In summary, the value and uniqueness of human capital will give rise to different employment modes and related HRM policies/configurations:

• *High on value of human capital and high on uniqueness*: The focus is on internal development of those employees that possess valuable and unique, organization-specific capabilities and skills. The company desires long-term commitment from these employees. Both the organization and the employees aim for mutual investment in order to cultivate and grow critical firm-specific skills. The HR configuration is based on establishing commitment through HRM practices such as extensive training, career development, and participation. The HR configuration for this employment mode resembles, to a large degree, the HRM practices that make up high performance work systems (see Chapter 4 on AMO, including a section on HPWS). Example: knowledge workers in high-tech firms.

• *High on value of human capital and low uniqueness*: Although these employees also add value to the organization, they are widely available in the labour market as they do not possess organization-specific skills. Instead of focusing on investment and internal development, the main employment mode is acquisition, i.e. 'buying' employees from the labour market who are instantly ready to contribute to the firm and who do not need to be invested in as their valuable skills have already been developed elsewhere. The HR configuration for this quadrant is mainly focused on staffing (recruitment, selection, on-boarding) and compared to the first employment mode, there is far less emphasis on investing in training and development. Examples: craftsmen like plumbers, electricians, and carpenters.

- *Low value of human capital and low uniqueness*: The human capital in this employment mode is of less strategic value and of a generic nature. In essence, it can be treated as a commodity and can easily be purchased from and returned to the labour market (Lepak & Snell, 1999, p. 39). The employment mode is focused on contracting and is transactional in nature: it simply focuses on short-term economic exchanges. As far as the HR con-figuration is concerned, the main emphasis is on securing compliance with the terms and conditions of the agreed-upon contract. There will be hardly any investment in training or development activities and performance appraisal and rewards will be job-based with a narrow focus on the quality and quantity of the work as agreed (Lepak & Snell, 1999, p. 40). Examples: temporary workers, maintenance staff.
- *Low value of human capital and high uniqueness*: Albeit that this kind of human capital is unique, it does not directly contribute to added value. This might have to do with its limited use by the firm (for example, hiring a lawyer for a specific issue), or because for value to be generated, parties need to work together in order to generate a jointly shared outcome. Lepak and Snell (1999, p. 41) use the concept of alliance to refer to a kind of hybrid employment mode that blends externalization and internalization. As working together implies combining knowledge, sharing information, trust and reciprocity, the employment relationship is based on partner-ship. The HR configuration consists of activities such as team building, process facilitation, communication, exchange programs, job rotation, and mentoring, in order to improve trust and encourage information sharing. Examples: lawyers, IT-specialists.

A, B and C Players: Accounting for Individuals Who Make Extra-ordinary Firm-level Contributions

Finally, a third model that focuses on differentiation. This model identifies 'A', 'B', and 'C' functions and players. As indicated, employees differ in their contribution towards implementing the business strategy, realizing strategic objectives, and hence achieving or helping to maintain sustainable competitive advantage. To put it more colloquially: some employees provide a bigger bang for the company's buck than others. Huselid, Beatty, and Becker (2005) build upon the theorizing of Lepak and Snell (1999) by identifying systematically the strategically important 'A' positions, which preferably should be filled by 'A' players.

In line with this thinking, Huselid et al. (2005) develop a portfolio approach to workforce management by identifying first the strategic positions (A positions) – those positions that contribute most to strategy and competitive advantage – and making sure that these are being fulfilled by the best possible employees (A players) and, secondly, that these are accompanied by good performers (B players) in essential support positions (B positions). The final step is making sure that non-performing employees (C players) and positions/ jobs (C positions) that do not add value are 'eliminated'.

The question then arises: how to identify those A positions? As indicated by Huselid et al. (2005, p. 111), economists and HR managers differ in that respect. Economists simply base this on the wages that someone is earning, thus, the most important jobs are those held by the most highly-paid employees. That situation is, however, a reflection of the past and might not be correct for the (near) future, and that is what strategy is all about. As far as HR managers are concerned, they also consider the level of skill or education, position in the hierarchy and responsibility. Yet again, however, this is a reflection of the past. In order to identify an appropriate and future-orientated identification of A positions, Huselid et al. (2005) recommend the following procedure.

First of all, line- and HR managers need to have a clear idea of the organization's strategy. Is the firm aiming for growth, innovation, cost leadership, quality, service, or a niche strategy? Based on the chosen strategy, management needs to identify the organization's critical capabilities, also called 'core competences'. These encompass finance, logistics, technology, information, and skills in order to convert the chosen strategy into a living reality. Based on this, the following question can then be posed: '… what jobs are critical to employing those capabilities in the execution of the strategy' (Huselid et al., 2005, p. 111)? Secondly, those jobs identified should be characterized by a high degree of so-called *performance variability*, as this represents potential for improving performance as well as the risk of not being able to perform well as a company. Examples of these include sales positions or the position of the purchasing manager in a low-cost retail chain. In both cases, performance can vary greatly either positively or negatively. As far as the B positions and B players are concerned, they are important as well as they support the A positions. The various positions and their defining characteristics are presented in Figure 6.1 (Huselid et al., 2005, p. 112).

	A Position STRATEGIC	B Position SUPPORT	C Position SURPLUS
DEFINING CHARACTERISTICS	Has a direct strategic impact AND Exhibits high performance variability among those in the position, representing upside potential	Has an indirect strategic impact by supporting strategic positions and minimizes downside risk by providing a foundation for strategic efforts. OR Has a potential strategic impact, but exhibits little performance variability among those in the position	May be required for the firm to function but has little strategic impact
Scope of authority	Autonomous decision making	Specific processes or procedures typically must be followed	Little discretion in work
Primary determinant of compensation	Performance	Job level	Market price
Effect on value creation	Creates value by substantially enhancing revenue or reducing costs	Supports value-creating positions	Has little positive economic impact
Consequences of mistakes	May be very costly, but missed revenue opportunities are a greater loss to the firm	May be very costly and can destroy value	Not necessarily costly
Consequences of hiring wrong person	Significant expense in terms of lost training investment and revenue opportunities	Fairly easily remedied through hiring of replacement	Easily remedied through hiring of replacement

Note: Reprinted from '"A players" or "A positions"?' by M. A. Huselid, R. W. Beatty, & B. E Becker, 2005, *Harvard Business Review*, 83, p. 112 (https://hbr.org/2005/12/a-players-or-a-positions-the-strategic-logic-of-workforce-management). Copyright 2005 by Harvard Business School Publishing Corporation.

Figure 6.1   Positions and characteristics

6.   ETHICAL CONSIDERATIONS

Reflecting on the various approaches towards differentiating the workforce based on uniqueness, potential for competitive advantage, and generating added value, we can also oppose this kind of thinking by simply referring to the moral obligation of offering decent work and jobs to people for which they get rewarded in a just and fair way. Sometimes the highly-paid jobs (belonging to the core, or those labelled as an A position, or workers positioned in the first strategic configuration of Lepak & Snell (1999)) are not that critical at all. Think of the recent COVID-19 pandemonium, during which qualified nurses fulfilled the most critical functions in hospitals and nursing homes, while working in an extremely contagious environment. Who is really crucial for a competitive advantage? Is it the pilot of an aeroplane or the flight attendant serving a passenger? Sometimes lower-paid jobs prove to be more essential than an executive function. Think of the parcel couriers who are the only point of contact with customers of an online shop. We need to be aware of the fact that reward systems and the kind of distribution, and equity they display, is also a reflection of the culture and values of an organization. In this respect, differentiation of the workforce and related consequences for compensation should not only be based on market or added value, but just as much based on values such as equity, fairness, and distributive justice.

REFERENCES

Atkinson, J. (1984). Manpower strategies for flexible organisations. *Personnel Management*, 16(8), 28–31.

Barney, J. B. (1991). Firm resources and sustained competitive advantage. *Journal of Management*, 17(1), 99–120. https://doi.org/10.1177%2F014920639101700108.

Becker, G. S. (1993). *Human Capital: A Theoretical and Empirical Analysis, with Special Reference to Education* (3rd ed.). Chicago: University of Chicago Press.

Becker, G. S. (1964). *Human Capital: A Theoretical and Empirical Analysis, with Special Reference to Education*. Cambridge, MA: National Bureau of Economic Research.

Boon, C., Eckardt, R., Lepak, D. P., & Boselie, P. (2018). Integrating strategic human capital and strategic human resource management. *The International Journal of Human Resource Management*, 29(1), 34–67. https:// doi .org/ 10 .1080/ 09585192 .2017.1380063.

Donate, M. J., Pena, I., & Sanchez de Pablo, J. D. (2016). HRM practices for human and social capital development: Effects on innovation capabilities. *International Journal of Human Resource Management*, 29(9), 928–953. https://doi.org/10.1080/09585192.2015.1047393.

Estevez-Abe, M., Iversen, T., & Soskice, D. (2001). Social protection and the formation of skills: A reinterpretation of the welfare state. In P. A. Hall, & D. Soskice (eds), *Varieties of Capitalism: The Institutional Foundations of Comparative Advantage* (pp. 145–183). Oxford: Oxford University Press.

Hitt, M. A., Biermant, L., Shimizu, K., & Kochhar, R. (2001). Direct and moderating effects of human capital on strategy and performance in professional service firms: A resource-based perspective. *Academy of Management Journal*, 44(1), 13–28. https://doi.org/10.5465/3069334.

Huselid, M. A., Beatty, R. W., & Becker, B. E. (2005). 'A players' or 'A positions'? *Harvard Business Review*, 83(12), 110–117. https://hbr.org/2005/12/a-players-or-a-positions-the-strategic-logic-of-workforce-management.

Lepak, D. P., & Snell, S. A. (1999). The human resource architecture: Toward a theory of human capital allocation and development. *Academy of Management Review*, 24(1), 31–48. https://doi.org/10.5465/amr.1999.1580439.

McCracken, M., McIvor, R., Treacy, R., & Wall, T. (2017). *Human Capital Theory: Assessing the Evidence for the Value and Importance of People to Organisational Success* (CIPD Technical Report). Retrieved from https://www.cipd.co.uk/Images/human-capital-theory-assessing-the-evidence_tcm18-22292.pdf.

Mincer, J. (1958). Investment in human capital and personal income distribution. *The Journal of Political Economy*, 66(44), 281–302. https://doi.org/10.1086/258055.

Ployhart, R. E., & Moliterno, T. P. (2011). Emergence of the human capital resource: A multilevel model. *Academy of Management Review*, 36(1), 127–150. https://doi.org/10.5465/amr.2009.0318.

Ployhart, R. E., Nyberg, A. J., Reily, G., & Maltarich, M. A. (2014). Human capital is dead: Long live human capital resources! *Journal of Management*, 40(2), 371–398. https://doi.org/10.1177/0149206313512152.

Schultz, T. W. (1961). Investment in human capital. *The American Economic Review*, 51(1), 1–17. https://www.jstor.org/stable/1818907.

Subramony, M. (2009). A meta-analytic investigation of the relationship between HRM bundles and firm performance. *Human Resource Management*, 48(5), 745–768. https://doi.org/10.1002/hrm.20315.

Vidal-Salazar, M., Hurtardo-Torres, N., & Mathis-Reche, F. (2012). Training as a generator of employee capabilities. *International Journal of Human Resource Management*, 23(13), 2680–2697. https://doi.org/10.1080/09585192.2011.610971.

Wright, P. M., & McMahan, G. C. (2011). Exploring human capital: Putting 'human' back into strategic human resource management. *Human Resource Management Journal*, 21(2), 93–104. https://doi.org/10.1111/j.1748-8583.2010.00165.x.

7.   Strength of the HRM system

TRIGGER

Imagine a large financial organization which has gone through a lot of turmoil during the financial economic crisis of which the bankruptcy of the Lehmann Brothers in September 2008 formed the starting point. The crisis itself led to a change in top management, substantial help by the government in order to maintain its solvability position, the selling of activities, etc. Instead of an engaged and motivated workforce fully trusting top management, morale went down, replacing trust with mistrust, etc. Would HRM be able to help recover the situation and bring back the once famous winning performance culture? That would need a tour de force. One of these financial institutions managed to do so by developing a 'strong' HRM system.

1.   DEFINING THE CONCEPT AND HOW IT CAN HELP PRACTITIONERS

The strength of the HRM system is a theory that focuses on creating strong situations (Mischel, 1973). Strong situations imply that people perceive a situation in the same way, which will generate uniform expectations about appropriate responses and behaviours. Their theory is not about the content of an HRM system, which will differ per organization and/or sector, dependent on the strategic perspective of the firm, but focuses on the underlying process mechanisms. In this respect, the HRM system – defined as a bundle of coherent HRM practices – is considered from the perspective of sending out signals to employees that '… allow them to understand the desired and appropriate responses and form a collective sense of what is expected' (Bowen & Ostroff, 2004, p. 204).

Focusing on the strength of an HRM system will in this way contribute to the performance of the firm. The strength of the HRM system creates the link between the 'what' of HR practices and the 'intent' or the 'why' of HR practices by focusing on the process of how it comes across to the employees (Ostroff & Bowen, 2016, p. 200). Three so-called meta-features of the Strength of the HRM system form together the process dimension of the HRM system: distinctiveness, consistency, and consensus. These three features enable the creation of a strong situation in the form of a shared meaning about the content among managers and employees, ultimately leading to organizational performance (Bowen & Ostroff, 2004, p. 206).

2.   FOUNDING FATHERS/MOTHERS

David Bowen and Cheri Ostroff have developed the strength of the HRM system theory. Their ideas were published in 2004 in the *Academy of Management Review* (AMR), one of the top journals in the field of management, focusing on theory development. Their ideas were quickly embraced by the academic community in the form of follow-up papers, either testing the proposed ideas of their theory or aimed at further development of their ideas. In 2005, they received the best paper award from the HR Division of the Academy of Management as a first indication of the excellent and valuable contribution of their work to theory development in the field of HRM. In 2014, they received the AMR decade award, indicating the most downloaded paper from all papers published in AMR in 2004. A better indication of quality, interest, and follow-up is hardly thinkable/conceivable. Reflecting on this award, in 2016, they published their paper 'Is there strength in the construct of HR system strength', in which they discuss consistencies and inconsistencies in their theoretical framework and offer a range of suggestions for further development of their theory. Needless to mention that we made good use of both their 2004 as well as their 2016 paper for writing this concise overview and how it can help practitioners.

Cheri Ostroff is a research professor at the School of Management, University of South Australia (Australia). David Bowen has a chair at the Thunderbird School of Global Management, Arizona State University (USA).

3.   CONTENT OF THE THEORY[1]

Bowen and Ostroff (2004) start from the premise that HR practices can be considered as signals to employees about the kind of responses and behaviours that are expected, rewarded, and valued. This is the very start of psychological climate perceptions. However, the interpretation of the practices can or will be different for each person, so these signals and their interpretation do not yet create a shared organizational climate. This implies that we need more to make sure that there will be a sense of common understanding among employees. Bowen and Ostroff call this a strong HRM system, for which they have identified nine different process mechanisms, grouped under the headings of three meta-features, being distinctiveness, consistency, and consensus. These three features have been derived from attribution theory (Kelley, 1967) and the theory on strong situations (Mischel, 1973, 1977).

- *Distinctiveness.* This implies that a situation (for example a set of HR practices) stands out from the broader environment; that it is able to draw attention and will arouse interest (Bowen & Ostroff, 2004, p. 208). For this to happen, the following four mechanisms are important: visibility of the HR practices, understandability of the HR practices, relevance of these practices for achieving both strategic as well as individual goals, and legitimacy/authority of the HR function (Ostroff & Bowen, 2016, p. 197).
- *Consistency.* This refers to the importance of consistency across time and across cause-and-effect relationships. More specifically, Bowen and Ostroff distinguish three mechanisms: *Instrumentality*, implying unambiguous cause-effects relationships between the desired content-focused behaviours (as desired by the HRM system) and associated consequences for employees; *validity* in the sense that HRM practices must have consistency between what they claim to do and what they actually do; and finally *consistency in HRM messages.* The latter encompasses different forms of consistency, such as making sure that there is consistency between what senior managers say the goals and values of the organization are and whether employees conclude the same based on their perceptions of HR practices. Bowen and Ostroff give the following example: 'managers may espouse a value of risk taking, but employees may infer that performance appraisal and reward system practices reinforce playing it safe' (Bowen & Ostroff, 2004, p. 211). Another form of consistency is the internal alignment across HRM practices, better known as internal fit. A well-known example in this respect is that if people are screened during selection for being able to work in teams (as the company is a typical team-based organization) then rewarding according to a group-based performance scheme will add to consistency. A final form of consistency relates to consistency over time. When HR practices have been in place for a long time (for example the habit of paying overtime for working during the weekends), this will add to agreement among the workers. (In addition, it will create strong reactions the very moment management wants to abolish this reward practice!)
- *Consensus.* This relates to the agreement among principal HRM decision makers, such as top, line- and HR managers and the degree of fairness of HR practices. Agreement among these decision makers will help to build consensus among employees, as they will be receiving similar communications and cues. In this respect, it will also help if there is close interaction among top-, line-, and HR managers (Bowen & Ostroff, 2004, p. 212). Fairness will be achieved by simultaneously paying attention to

distributive justice, procedural justice, and interactional justice ('managers explaining openly and respectfully to employees the reason behind decisions and the distribution of outcomes', Bowen & Ostroff, 2004, p. 212).

These nine dimensions together make up the strength of the HRM system and will help to build shared perceptions in a unit or organization. HRM will be able to send unambiguous messages about priorities, values, and climate. Moreover, it will help to create a strong organizational climate for a particular strategic focus, thereby aligning the HRM system with the strategic perspective of the organization and contributing to strengthening the HRM-performance link (Ostroff & Bowen, 2016, p. 197). Below we summarize this theory about the Strength of the HRM system, see Figure 7.1.

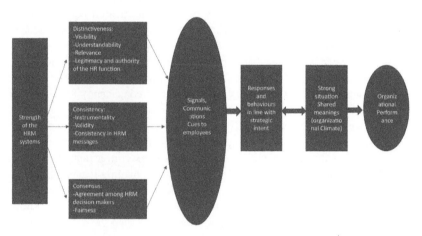

Figure 7.1   Summarizing the theory about the Strength of the HRM system

4.   EMPIRICAL EVIDENCE: USAGE, EFFECTS, RESULTS

In their 2004 theoretical paper, in which they unfold and build the theory of the Strength of the HRM system, Bowen and Ostroff make a number of promises in the form of propositions what we can expect once we have managed to create a strong HRM system. These are as follows:

- a strong HRM system '… will foster the emergence of an organizational climate (collective, shared perceptions) from psychological climates (individual level perceptions);

- ... In turn, organizational climate will display a significant association with employee attitudes and behaviours;
- ... a strong HRM system can enhance organizational performance owing to shared meanings in promotion of collective responses that are consistent with organizational strategic goals' (Bowen & Ostroff, 2004, p. 213).

What has come true in the past 15 years? Do we have evidence that a strong HRM system can produce the kind of effects as proposed in 2004? The authors themselves are surprised, not to say overwhelmed, by the abundance of fellow academics having made use of their theorizing since its publication in 2004. Yet they indicate that many researchers – despite having made use of the concept of HRM system strength – have not really tested it. Very often, reference to the concept has been made either for building theoretical rationales (Nishii, Lepak, & Schneider, 2008) or for interpreting empirical results (Ostroff & Bowen, 2016, p. 197). Examples of such interpretations are Hong, Liao, Hu, and Jiang (2013), with respect to being able to explain stronger relationships between service climate and service outcomes and Veld, Paauwe, & Boselie (2010), who use the theory for providing reasons why shared perceptions of the content of the HR systems positively influence climate in hospitals (climates for safety and quality) and other HR outcomes, such as commitment (see also Ostroff & Bowen, 2016, p. 198).

Many academics have tested their ideas by measuring perceptions of the nine dimensions at the individual level and linking these to individual attitudes and outcomes. A good example in this respect is the study by Delmotte et al. (2012), who did an excellent job in operationalizing the nine dimensions. Just like in many other studies, Delmotte et al. (2012) treated it as an individual level difference variable, while Bowen and Ostroff explicitly have developed the HRM Strength concept as a higher-level contextual variable. According to Sanders et al. (2014), until now a comprehensive and sophisticated measure of HRM system strength has not yet been developed (Ostroff & Bowen, 2016, p. 199). However, many researchers have opted for measuring the dimensions of system strength at the individual level. Subsequently they checked for the degree of similarity, justifying aggregation and then were able to draw conclusions about the effect of these shared perceptions of the meaning of HR practices (very often called climate) on all kinds of HR related outcomes, such as commitment (positive) and intention to quit (negative). Overall, there seems to be enough empirical support for the role of HRM System Strength for shaping shared meanings, collective responses and thus contributing to important HR and organizational outcomes. In this respect, Ostroff and Bowen (2016, p. 200) refer to Den Hartog et al. (2013); Katou et al. (2014); Li et al. (2011); Ribeiro et al. (2011); and Sanders et al. (2008) for examples.

Therefore, the promises in the form of propositions in their 2004 paper have more or less materialized, despite methodological shortcomings as indicated by Ostroff and Bowen themselves. In this respect, we must admit that it is difficult to label the Strength of the HRM System as a tested theory. There are still many directions for future research and especially the central concept of HRM Strength as a higher-level contextual variable has not yet been properly operationalized or empirically tested. However, we dare to speak of a 'proven' theory in the sense of a theory that helps to clarify process dimensions that play an important role in the relationship between HRM and performance. Moreover, the nine dimensions are easy to understand and – once applied – will help practitioners/HR- and line managers to create strong situations.

5.   A FINAL WARNING AND AN OPTIMISTIC NOTE

Ostroff and Bowen (2016, p. 205) end their reflection on 15 years of research with the remark that there is also a downside to creating a strong climate (with the help of a strong HRM system), which is groupthink. Too much consensus and sharing the same values and responding in the same way to events, can jeopardize independent thinking and can hinder expressing constructive criticism. The focus might become too inward directed and less open to external changes in the marketplace or sector and what these might imply for the continuity of the organization.

On a more positive note, they hint to a more integral perspective in which dimensions such as distinctiveness, consistency, and consensus, as favoured in the strength of the HRM system, are combined with similar signals emanating from business functions such as marketing, operations, and the services cape[2] (see also Bowen and Schneider, 2014). Recent reviews also provide evidence that shared employees' perceptions of the HR practices can be linked – in a positive way – to the attitudes and perceptions of customers via a strong climate (for example for service), in this way contributing to firm performance (for a review of those linkages, see: Bowen & Schneider, 2014; Hong et al., 2013).

More generally, the theory of Strength of the HRM System forms part of an important stream in HRM theory development, which is the so-called 'process' stream. Next to content (the 'what' in the form of the different HRM practices), the process approach focuses on the underlying process dimensions. An important stream/line of thinking that has contributed to solving the black box between HRM practices and outcomes such as performance and well-being.

NOTES

1. This section is based on Bowen and Ostroff (2004) and on Ostroff and Bowen (2016).
2. *Servicescape* is a model developed by Booms and Bitner (1981) to emphasize the impact of the physical environment in which a service process takes place (www.wikipedia.com).

REFERENCES

Booms, B.H. and Bitner, M.J. (1981) Marketing Strategies and Organization Structures for Service Firms. In: *Marketing of Services, American Marketing Association,* Chicago, 47-51.
Bowen, D. E., & Ostroff, C. (2004). Understanding HRM-firm performance linkages: The role of the "strength" of the HRM system. *Academy of Management Review,* 29(2), 203–221. https://doi.org/10.5465/amr.2004.12736076.
Bowen, D. E., & Schneider, B. (2014). A service climate synthesis and future research agenda. *Journal of Service Research,* 17(1), 5–22. https://doi.org/10.1177%2F1094670513491633.
Delmotte, J., De Winne, S., & Sels, L. (2012). Towards an assessment of perceived HRM system strength: Scale development and validation. *The International Journal of Human Resource Management,* 23(7), 1481–1506. https:// doi .org/ 10 .1080/ 09585192.2011.579921.
Den Hartog, D. N., Boon, C., Verburg, R. M., Croon, M. A. (2013). HRM, communication, satisfaction, and perceived performance: A cross-level test. *Journal of Management,* 39(6),1637–1665. https://doi.org/10.1177/0149206312440118.
Hong, Y., Liao, H., Hu, J., & Jiang, K. 2013. Missing link in the service profit chain: A meta-analytic review of the antecedents, consequences, and moderators of service climate. *Journal of Applied Psychology,* 98, 237–267. https:// doi .org/ 10 .1037/ a0031666.
Katou, A. A., Budhwar, P. S., & Patel, C. (2014). Content vs. process in the HRM-performance relationship: An empirical examination. *Human Resource Management,* 53(4), 527–544. https://doi.org/10.1002/hrm.21606.
Kelley, H. H. (1967). Attribution theory in social psychology. In D. Levine (ed.), *Nebraska Symposium on Motivation* (pp. 192–240). Lincoln, NE: University of Nebraska Press.
Li, X., Frenkel, S. J., & Sanders, K. (2011). Strategic HRM as process: How HR system and organizational climate strength influence Chinese employee attitudes. *The International Journal of Human Resource Management,* 22(9), 1825–1842. https:// doi.org/10.1080/09585192.2011.573965.
Mischel, W. (1973). Toward a cognitive social learning reconceptualization of personality. *Psychological Review,* 80(4), 252–283. https://doi.org/10.1037/h0035002.
Mischel, W. (1977). On the future of personality measurement. *American Psychologist,* 32(4), 246–254. https://doi.org/10.1037/0003-066X.32.4.246.
Nishii, L. H., Lepak, D. P., & Schneider, B. (2008). Employee attributions of the "why" of HR practices: Their effects on employee attitudes and behaviors, and customer satisfaction. *Personnel Psychology,* 61(3), 503–545. https://doi.org/10.1111/j.1744 -6570.2008.00121.x.

Ostroff, C., & Bowen, D. E. (2016). Reflections on the 2014 decade award: Is there strength in the construct of HR system strength? *Academy of Management Review*, 41(2), 196–214. https://doi.org/10.5465/amr.2015.0323

Ribeiro, T. R., Coelho, J. P., & Gomes, J. F. S. (2011). HRM strength, situation strength and improvisation behavior. *Management Research*, 9(2), 118–136. https://doi.org/10.1108/1536-541111155245.

Sanders, K., Dorenbosch, L., & de Reuver, R. (2008). The impact of individual and shared employee perceptions of HRM on affective commitment. Considering climate strength. *Personnel Review*, 37(4), 412–425. https:// doi .org/ 10 .1108/ 00483480810877589.

Sanders, K., Shipton, H., & Gomes, J. F. S. (2014). Guest editor's introduction: Is the HRM process important? Past, current, and future challenges. *Human Resource Management*, 53(4), 489–503. https://doi.org/10.1002/hrm.21644.

Veld, M., Paauwe, J., & Boselie, P. (2010). HRM and strategic climates in hospitals: Does the message come across at the ward level? *Human Resource Management Journal*, 20(4), 339–356. https://doi.org/10.1111/j.1748-8583.2010.00139.x.

8.   Well-being: the crucial link between HRM practices and outcomes

TRIGGER

We, as managers, as entrepreneurs, attract people to perform a service or help to develop, produce, and sell a product, for which we pay them (hopefully) a decent amount of money and treat them with the right leadership style, working conditions, and opportunities to develop themselves. Productivity, performance will increase, if people are being treated well. However, well-being is not just a means to an end, it is also a goal in itself, which we owe to our responsibility as managers and leaders for dealing with people in a decent, fair, and dignified way. This double-edged sword of well-being makes it an extremely important topic which, next to performance, should be on top of mind for every line- and HR manager.

1.   ON THE IMPORTANCE OF WELL-BEING

As indicated above, well-being at work is important in its own right. It is a value, an objective to aim at irrespective of the nature of work, the kind of workers involved, or the conditions under which work is carried out. At the same time, it is also important as a means to an end. Taking care of well-being has positive economic and social consequences both at organizational and societal levels. The International Labour Organization (ILO) emphasizes the importance of well-being: 'Workplace Wellbeing relates to all aspects of working life, from the quality and safety of the physical environment, to how workers feel about their work, their working environment, the climate at work and work organization. The aim of measures for workplace well-being is to complement occupational safety and health measures to make sure workers are safe, healthy, satisfied and engaged at work. Workers' well-being is a key factor in determining an organization's long-term effectiveness. Many studies show a direct link between productivity levels and the general health and well-being of the workforce' (ILO, n.d.).

Positive consequences such as lower stress, fewer absences due to illness, lower staff turnover and … higher productivity or stronger service orientation to customers due to better committed people. The fact that within less than one second Google generates more than 4,460,000,000 hits on the concept of 'well-being at work' gives an impression of the importance and omnipresence of the concept.

2.　　DEFINING THE CONCEPT AND ITS RELEVANCE FOR PRACTITIONERS

It is impossible to indicate a founding father or mother of a dominant theory on well-being as the concept – just like performance – is used a lot. Numerous academic disciplines consider well-being a core concept in their domain of knowledge. Think of organizational behaviour, work and organizational psychology, and human resource studies, just to mention a few. This also implies that each discipline has its own definition of well-being. Here we opt for the definition by Warr (1987, 2002), which emphasizes the psychological or subjective perspective on well-being at work: the overall quality of an individual's subjective experience and functioning at work. This is still a rather abstract definition. More specific is the one by Grant et al. (2007). They distinguish three dimensions of well-being:

- Happiness, which refers to one's individual experience at work and covers positive worker attitudes which can be expressed in terms of affective commitment and job satisfaction.
- Health related well-being, which includes on the one hand strain-related aspects of health such as stress, burn-out, and exhaustion, and on the other hand (on a more positive note), work engagement.
- Relationship well-being, which focuses on interactions and the quality of relationships between employees and between employees and managers/ organization. Once positive, a trusting relationship and effective collaboration will be the result.

3.　　THEORETICAL INSIGHTS

Vitamin Model

One of the most attractive and practical theories to influence the degree of well-being is the so-called Vitamin model by Warr (2002), which uses the analogy of the useful effects of vitamins. The focus of this theory is on characteristics of the work environment and job features such as job design and degree of control over one's work (autonomy). Below we present a list of these features which can promote well-being:

- Opportunity for control/personal influence.

- Opportunity to use own abilities/skills.
- Having challenging demands/goals.
- Job variety.
- Role/environmental clarity.
- Availability of money (being paid well for what you do).
- Opportunity for social interaction/interpersonal contact.
- Physical security/safe work environment.
- Having a job that you value.
- Supportive supervision.
- Good career prospects and job security.
- Fair treatment.

The analogy with vitamins is as follows. The more these job features are present in the work setting, the higher the degree of well-being. However – just like with vitamins – the effect of 'the more the better' has its limits and can even turn into reversed, negative effects on well-being. For example: variety in the job is good, but too much variety can imply too many demands upon one's capabilities or too much chaos in one's job. Same for autonomy: a certain degree of autonomy is good, but too much might imply not knowing what to do, lack of direction, feeling oneself at a loss, etc.

Job Demands-Resources Model (JDR Model)

Jobs have different job characteristics, which can have a large impact upon the well-being of employees. According to Bakker and Demerouti (2007), these characteristics, which are very specific per job, can be classified into two general categories: job demands and job resources. *Job demands*, such as work pressure '… are the physical, psychological, social or organizational aspects of the job, that require sustained physical and/or psychological effort or skill' (Bakker & Demerouti, 2007, p. 312). *Job resources*, on the other hand, such as coaching by your supervisor, autonomy, constructive feedback, and career opportunities, refer to '… those physical, psychological, social or organiza-tional aspects of the job that are either/or: functional in achieving work goals; reduce job demands and the associated physiological and psychological cost; stimulate personal growth, learning and development' (Bakker & Demerouti, 2007, p. 312). So, job resources help cope with the demands arising out of the workplace and this balance can result in well-being, engagement, or in the case of a non-balance, it will result in either stress, exhaustion (not enough resources to cope with the demands), or boredom (too many resources avail-able, but a lack of challenging demands). A more extensive treatment of the JDR model can be found in Chapter 10 of this book.

Other Theoretical Perspectives

- Social exchange theory and norm of reciprocity (felt obligation): if workers are satisfied with their job because of good working conditions, fair treatment, and the received benefits, they feel committed to the organization and are more likely to return the favours by working hard and in a dedicated way. In this way, it will enhance the effectiveness and performance of the organization (Peccei et al., 2013).
- Broaden & Build (B&B) theory: being satisfied and happy, *broadens* a person's interest and will promote creative behaviour aimed at discovery, developing new ideas, and social bonds. Consecutively, these more novel, varied, and exploratory ideas and actions help to *build* new physical, intellectual, and social resources. This generates a positive attitude/mindset, increased well-being and will contribute to both better in-role and extra-role behaviour (Frederickson, 2001; Peccei et al., 2013).
- 'Feeling good–doing good' arguments: put simply, once people are in a positive mood, they are more inclined to engage in altruistic and helping behaviour. That kind of helping behaviour is especially important in service contexts, where it can make a significant difference in customer satisfaction and thus in overall service performance (George & Brief, 1992; Peccei & Rosenthal, 2001).
- Emotional contagion theory: the name of the theory itself is indicative of its meaning, both in a positive as well as a negative sense. Employees that have a positive mood transmit these positive feelings not only to colleagues, while interacting with them, but also to customers with which they are in direct contact. This will lead to more positive customer evaluations. By word-of-mouth promotion this will increase sales. In short, this theory of emotional contagion refers to the transfer of positive or negative emotions from one person to the other and the tendency, according to Pugh (2001) for interacting individuals to converge emotionally (Peccei et al., 2013). So, be warned, negative emotions can also be transferred, which in the end might result in so-called 'toxic' workplaces.
- Conservation of resources (COR) theory: this theory by Hobfoll (1989) is linked to the Job Demands Resources theory. Resources such as job control (autonomy), social support, and job security are valued in their own right as they '… contribute to the achievement of positive personal outcomes such as better coping, adaptation and well-being' (Peccei et al., 2013, p. 27). According to Hobfoll and Freedy (1993), employees who possess more resources (such as task discretion and social support) and who work in a resource-rich setting will more likely experience positive well-being outcomes and are less likely to experience negative outcomes such as stress and exhaustion.

4. EMPIRICAL EVIDENCE/OUTCOMES

Various disciplines have carried out research into the factors/variables which have a positive effect on well-being and performance. The direction of causality (what causes what?) is not always clear. One can imagine that a well-performing team (for example your favourite football or hockey team) feels great and experiences a sense of well-being after a victory. Think of expressions such as 'being in a winning mood' or 'never change a winning team'. It is best to think of it as an iterative cycle, where well-being contributes to increased performance, which, once sustained, contributes to increased well-being or the sustenance of it.[1] This is all summarized in the 'The happy worker–productive worker thesis, which states that employees high in well-being also perform well, and vice versa' (Wright & Cropanzano, 2000). Based on 84 quantitative studies, published from 2003 to 2015, Nielsen et al. (2017) carried out a review and meta-analysis with the following key research issue: which type of resources are most important in predicting both employee well-being and performance at various levels of analysis? In their analysis, both HRM practices and well-being, as well as organizational performance, are included.

All 84 studies are based on empirical data collected in different organizations across the globe at different levels of analysis (individual, group, leader, and organizational levels). The various indicators used to measure well-being are as follows: job satisfaction, happiness, organizational commitment, intention to remain with the organization, work engagement, sense of purpose, and affective wellbeing (Nielsen et al., 2017). Based on their review study we highlight the following results.

- 'The individual resources most often studied in relation to both employee well-being and performance were the four resources of self-efficacy,[2] hope, optimism, and resilience that together form Psychological Capital' (Nielsen et al., 2017, p. 110). More recently, job crafting was also present a lot. Job crafting refers to the alterations employees make to their work in order to change the task, relational, and cognitive boundaries of their work (Wrzesniewski & Dutton, 2001).
- At the group level, the most prominently present resources were social support and the fit between the group and the person.
- At the level of the leaders, the most prominent factors were transformational leadership, supervisory social support, and Leader-Member Exchange (LMX). The latter implies having good quality relationships between a leader and employees (Graen & Uhl-Bien, 1995).
- The organizational resource most often explored was autonomy. Next, HRM practices, quite often studied as a cluster of practices or separately

such as compensation-based schemes, training, career supporting activities, and performance appraisals. 'This evidence is often outlined in terms of the mutual gains perspective of HRM, according to which HR practices are associated with benefits for both employees (e.g., through enhanced job satisfaction) and the organization (e.g., through workplace productivity)' (Nielsen et al., 2017, p. 113).

Summarizing their results, Nielsen et al. (2017) '… found that resources at all four levels were significantly related to both employee well-being and performance. Our results, therefore, suggest that interventions focused on any of these resources, and potentially in combination, will be successful in improving both employee well-being and performance' (p. 117).

5.   INTERVENTIONS, WHAT TO DO?

Different routes, preferably called employee pathways, are possible to influence well-being and performance. The empirical review in the previous section has discussed a variety of resources operating at different levels of analyses, such as individual, group, leader, and organizational levels. Next to well-being, we have witnessed in the chapter on the AMO model, how important HRM practices are, once they are focused on improving Abilities,

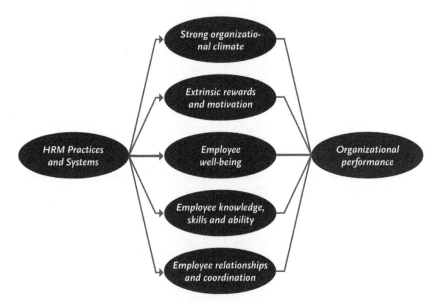

Figure 8.1   Alternative employee-related pathways linking HRM and organizational performance

Motivation and strengthening the Opportunity for participation, voice (AMO model, see Chapter 4). In Figure 8.1, we depict different pathways, next to well-being, which can impact organizational performance. Preferably, these different pathways will be combined to strengthen the link with organizational performance.

Below we highlight two approaches,[3] which both offer a good overview of interventions/mechanisms in order to impact well-being and subsequent individual and organizational performance.

The first one (Figure 8.2) has been developed by R. Peccei (personal communication, 2019) and gives a good overview of possible interventions at individual level (job design), leadership level, and organizational level by emphasizing different HRM practices. Finally, the importance of clarity of goals (see chapter on goal setting) and the importance of a strong climate (see chapter on Strength of the HRM system) are emphasized. All these factors and policies culminate in a so-called High-Quality workplace and subsequently in a Happy workplace where the employee experiences mainly positive effects (such as job satisfaction, enthusiasm, engagement) and hardly any negative effects (such as lack of satisfaction, fatigue, stress, anxiety, burn-out).

The second one (Figure 8.3), developed by Guest (2017, p. 30) focuses on five sets of HRM practices, aimed at developing a 'positive' employment relationship through which well-being will thrive, see Figure 8.3.

The five sets of HRM practices are explained in Table 8.1. (Guest, 2017, p. 31).

Investing in people implies strengthening their competences, which generates feelings of security and will help the development of self-efficacy, which according to Guest (2017) is an important antecedent of well-being. The second set of HR practices focuses on providing engaging work. Earlier we mentioned the importance of autonomy and opportunities for control. Job design is crucial in this respect. The third set of HR practices encompasses a whole range of different measures, which all relate to fairness, justice, and psychological safety in the workplace, in order to create a positive social and physical environment. The importance of voice and participation is the focal point of attention in the fourth set of HR practices. Finally, organizational support through HR practices such as participative management, stimulating involvement, family-friendly work arrangement, and performance management systems focused on development (Guest, 2017).

Once these five sets of HR practices are in place, it will '… be associated with higher employee work-related well-being and a positive employment relationship. High well-being will be reflected in psychological and physical health and positive social relationships at work. A positive employment relationship will be reflected in high levels of trust, a sense of fairness, a feeling of

Note: Reprinted from King's College Lecture on well-being, by R. Peccei, 2019.

Figure 8.2   Model of the high-quality workplace

Figure 8.3   *HRM, well-being and the employment relationship, and performance*

security, a fulfilled psychological contract and a high quality of working life' (Guest, 2017, pp. 31–32), all depicted in Figure 8.3 (Guest, 2017, p. 30).

Both high well-being and a strong positive employment relationship will bring about individual and organizational performance. After all, high well-being will generate better health and more energy and, bearing in mind social exchange theory, employees will be more inclined to return the favours by working hard and in a dedicated way.

Table 8.1　　Provisional HR-practices designed to promote employee well-being

Investing in employees	Recruitment and selection Training and development Mentoring and career support
Providing engaging work	Jobs designed to provide autonomy and challenge Information provision and feedback Skill utilization
Positive social and physical environment	Health and safety a priority Equal opportunities/diversity management Zero tolerance for bullying and harassment Required and optional social interaction Fair collective reward/high basic pay Employment security/employability
Voice	Extensive two-way communication Employee surveys Collective representation
Organizational support	Participative/supportive management Involvement climate and practices Flexible and family-friendly work arrangements Developmental performance management

Note: Reprinted from 'Human resource management and employee well-being: Towards a new analytic framework', by D. E. Guest, 2017, *Human Resource Management Journal*, 27(1), p. 31 (https://doi.org/10.1111/1748-8583.12139). Copyright 2017 by John Wiley & Sons Ltd.

NOTES

1.　For a more informed and detailed discussion on the issue of causality between HRM, well-being and performance we refer to Peccei et al. (2013, pp. 16–45).
2.　Self-efficacy refers to an individual's belief in his or her capacity to execute behaviours necessary to produce specific performance attainments (Bandura, 1977, 1986).
3.　The reason for opting for the two approaches/models (one by Peccei (2019) and one by Guest (2017)) is that they not only offer an overview of possible interventions, which are important and feasible from a practitioners' point of view, but both are also integrating the findings and insights of this chapter in a useful framework with well-being at the heart of it.

REFERENCES

Bakker, A., & Demerouti, E. (2007). The job demands-resources model: State of the art. *Journal of Managerial Psychology*, 22(3), 309–328. https://doi.org/10.1108/02683940710733115.

Bandura, A. (1977). Self-efficacy: Toward a unifying theory of behavioral change. *Psychological Review*, 84(2), 191–215. https://doi.org/10.1037/0033-295X.84.2.191.

Bandura, A. (1986). Fearful expectations and avoidant actions as coeffects of perceived self-inefficacy. *American Psychologist*, 41(12), 1389–1391. https://doi.org/10.1037/0003-066X.41.12.1389

Frederickson, B. L. (2001). The role of positive emotions in positive psychology: The broaden-and-build theory of positive emotions. *American Psychologist*, 56(3), 218–226. https://doi.org/10.1037/0003-066X.56.3.218.

George, J. M., & Brief, A. P. (1992). Feeling good-doing good: A conceptual analysis of the mood at work-organizational spontaneity relationship. *Psychological Bulletin*, 112(2), 310–329. https://doi.org/10.1037/0033-2909.112.2.310.

Graen, G. B., & Uhl-Bien, M. (1995). Relationship-based approach to leadership: Development of leader member exchange (LMX) theory of leadership over 25 years: Applying multi-level multi-domain perspective. *The Leadership Quarterly*, 6(2), 219–247. https://doi.org/10.1016/1048-9843(95)90036-5.

Grant, A. M., Christianson, M. K., & Price, R. H. (2007). Happiness, health, or relationships? Managerial practices and employee well-being tradeoffs. *Academy of Management Executive*, 21(1), 51–63. https://doi.org/10.5465/amp.2007.26421238.

Guest, D. E. (2017). Human resource management and employee well-being: Towards a new analytic framework. *Human Resource Management Journal*, 27(1), 22–38. https://doi.org/10.1111/1748-8583.12139.

Hobfoll, S. E. (1989). Conservation of resources: A new attempt at conceptualizing stress. *American Psychologist*, 44(3), 513–524.

Hobfoll, S. E., & Freedy, J. (1993). Conservation of resources: A general stress theory applied to burnout. In W. B. Schaufeli, C. Maslach, & T. Marek (eds), *Professional Burnout: Recent Developments in Theory and Research* (pp. 115–129). Abingdon: Taylor & Francis.

International Labour Organization (ILO). (n.d.). *Workplace Well-being*. https://www.ilo.org/safework/areasofwork/workplace-health-promotion-and-well-being/WCMS_118396/lang--en/index.htm

Nielsen, K., Nielsen, M. B., Ogbonnaya, C., Känsälä, M., Saari, E., & Isaksson, K. (2017). Workplace resources to improve both employee well-being and performance: A systematic review and meta-analysis. *An International Journal of Work, Health & Organisations*, 31(2), 101–120. https://doi.org/10.1080/02678373.2017.1304463.

Peccei, R. (2019). Lecture on well-being at Kings' College. London.

Peccei, R., & Rosenthal, P. (2001). Delivering customer-oriented behaviour through empowerment: An empirical test of HRM assumptions. *Journal of Management Studies*, 38(6), 831–857. https://doi.org/10.1111/1467-6486.00261.

Peccei, R., van de Voorde, K., & van Veldhoven, M. (2013). HRM, well-being and performance: A theoretical and empirical review. In J. Paauwe, D. Guest, & P. Wright (eds), *HRM and Performance: Achievements and Challenges* (pp. 15–45). New York: Wiley.

Pugh, S. D. (2001). Service with a smile: Emotional contagion in the service encounter. *Academy of Management Journal*, 44(5), 1018–1027. https://doi.org/10.5465/3069445.Warr. P. B. (1987). *Work, Unemployment, and Mental Health*. Oxford: Clarendon Press.

Warr, P. (1987). *Work, unemployment, and mental health*. Oxford University Press.

Warr, P. (2002). The study of well-being, behaviour and attitudes. In P. Warr (ed.), *Psychology at Work* (pp. 1–25). London: Penguin Press.

Wright, T. A., & Cropanzano, R. (2000). Psychological well-being and job satisfaction as predictors of job performance. *Journal of Occupational Health Psychology*, 5(1), 84–94. https://doi.org/10.1037/1076-8998.5.1.84.

Wrzesniewski, A., & Dutton, J. E. (2001). Crafting a job: Revisioning employees as active crafters of their work. *Academy of Management Review*, 26(2), 179–201. https://doi.org/10.5465/amr.2001.4378011.

9.   Line management enactment

TRIGGER

Having been a line manager myself, I know that one must do their share of HRM activities, whether one likes it or not. Selection interviews, calibration meetings, appraisal interviews, solving conflicts between employees, writing proposals for promotion, etc. And ... one also has to react to all kind of proposals from the HR-Department. Sometimes that is a burden and sometimes they take great initiatives. My way of getting along with the HR Department is based on a simple kind of reasoning. Confronted with a proposal or a new initiative by HR, I simply ask myself the following questions:

- *Will it help me to better achieve the goals of my department?*
- *Will my employees, thanks to this initiative, increase their competencies (KSAs: knowledge, skills, and abilities)?*
- *Will my employees become more motivated, will they work harder, better, and display more effort?*
- *Will it enrich their opportunities for participation, voice, development, and well-being?*

I also put those questions forward to HR. If the answer to all four question is no, or if HR is not able to provide a convincing and satisfactory answer, then I simply refuse to cooperate. Apparently, these are the kind of lenses or glasses, through which line managers perceive the HR Department. Positive answers to the four questions imply implementation of HR activities thanks to the line manager's willingness to be involved, as he/she perceives the HR department as being effective and able to add value.

Below we highlight the topic of line management enactment in taking on HR activities, discussing the kind of factors which hinder or facilitate the involvement in carrying out HR activities, culminating in a framework which depicts the interaction between HR and line management, showing how it can help effective implementation and create an HR Department that truly adds value.

1.   DEFINING THE CONCEPT AND HOW IT CAN HELP PRACTITIONERS

The defining characteristics that distinguish traditional personnel management from strategic human resource management are the focus on aligning HRM with the business strategy, focus on return on investment instead of a focus on personnel costs, and the increased involvement of line managers in the management of human resources to achieve high commitment, high quality, and flexibility (Guest, 1989). Involvement of line managers implies the devolution of HRM practices from the HR department to line management. If successful, we call this *line-management enactment*, implying that they help to implement HRM practices, are willing to act as a role model, take the lead, and are even willing to control the proper execution of these HRM activities (for example, the introduction of a new performance appraisal system or a new system of performance related pay). Below we highlight this concept, including the hindering and favouring factors both from the perspective of the HR function as well as from the perspective of the line manager. In this way, we can help to create optimal conditions for a line manager to carry out HRM activities to the benefit of the goals of his/her department and to the benefit of the employees reporting to him/her.

2.   FOUNDING FATHERS/MOTHERS: MAIN AUTHORS ON THE TOPIC

With the rise of strategic HRM in the 1980s and 1990s, authors such as Storey, Guest, Purcell, Hutchinson, Marchington, Wilkinson, Ulrich, Wright, Nishii, Paauwe, and Boselie, were not only discussing the relationship between HRM and performance, but also the implementation of strategic HRM and the role of line managers. This implies that we cannot identify a founding father or mother, nor is there a real theory on line management enactment. It is more a number of insights, frameworks, and recommendations that can help line managers to become more effective in enacting HRM. Frameworks such as the process model of Wright and Nishii (2013) below, Strengths of the HRM system (see Chapter 7, this book) and AMO theory (see Chapter 4, this book) are an example of this. Additional insights are derived from Bos-Nehles (2010); Bos-Nehles et al. (2013); Knies and Leisink (2014), and more recently, Hewett and Shantz (2021).

3.   OVERVIEW/CONTENT/APPLICATIONS

The HR function in an organization is not only carried out by the HR department, but many others are also involved, including line managers, employees,
and outside vendors offering specialized services such as doing part of the
recruitment, training and development, or dealing with the payroll. Here we
focus on the interaction between the HR department and line management. In
2008, Nishii and Wright presented their process model of strategic HRM (see
also Wright & Nishii, 2013). They make a distinction between intended HR
practices, actual HR practices, perceived HR practices, employee reaction, and
organizational performance. Boselie and Paauwe (Personal Communication,
2010) have transformed this into the HR Value Chain (see Figure 9.1) in order
to indicate that with every link in the chain, something can go wrong, which
would lead to less added value or even the opposite of what was intended.

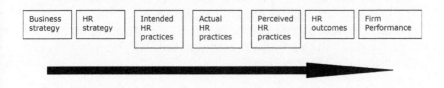

Figure 9.1   The HR value chain

Let us take the introduction of a new appraisal system. The HR department
designs this either with or without the help of a consultancy firm (intended
HR practice). Subsequently, there is the phase of implementation with the
involvement of line management. They might make some remarks for adapting
it and might be in need of further clarification or a training session in order to
understand and apply the new appraisal system (actual HR practices). Here we
might already run the risk that it will be implemented in a different way than
intended by the HR department or they might interpret it in a different way.
For example, HR wants to develop a system which is fair and does more justice
to those who work faster or smarter, whereas line management perceives it
as a new approach towards more exploitation of all workers or finds it too
complicated to work with. The next link in the HR Value Chain is the way in
which the workers perceive it (perceived HR practices). Their way of perceiv-
ing (positive, negative, neutral) will determine their attitudinal and subsequent
behavioural reaction (HR outcomes). If they go along with the negative
interpretation by their line manager as indicated above, the chances of them

reacting in a positive way will be minimal. In this way, we are again facing the risk that the intended HR practice does not live up to its promise or intended purpose. With every link in the chain, we run the risk of failure/damage. This implies that for an HR manager it is important to collaborate closely with line management (co-creation) as well as to keep their finger on the pulse in every part of the value chain.

Optimizing the HR Value Chain: Hindering and Favouring Factors

Based on an overview of empirical research, Guest and Bos-Nehles (2013) mention the following five factors, which hinder or further the proper imple-mentation of HR practices and thus the degree of line management enactment:

- Do line managers have the *desire* to carry out HRM responsibilities?
- Do they have enough *capacity/time* to be involved in personnel manage-ment activities next to their operational and strategic responsibilities?
- Do they have sufficient *HR related competences*?
- Do they get enough *support and advice* from their HR manager?
- Are the *policies and procedures* related to their HR responsibilities and practices *clear and user-friendly?*

The empirical evidence is mixed concerning these five factors. Capacity in the sense of having enough time is a serious issue, as is the lack of HR related competences. HR managers, especially, are often of the opinion that line man-agers do not want to carry out their HR responsibilities and are also lacking the required competences. Moreover, line managers might be inclined to bend the rules in order to make them fit their own needs for their own department, business, or unit, at least according to the opinion of the HR managers (see, for example, Bond & Wise, 2003; Harris, 2001; Sanders & Frenkel, 2011). However, some research reports different outcomes as they include the line managers' views on the five factors as indicated above (Bos-Nehles, 2010; Renwick, 2003). Line managers themselves report to have the desire and com-petence to carry out HR activities and that they get valuable advice and support from their HR manager as well as clear policies and procedures (Bos-Nehles, 2010; Guest & Bos-Nehles, 2013). The only lacking element appears to be capacity/time, set against their other operational activities, belonging to the core of their job. In this sense, Bos-Nehles depicts a remarkably more positive view on the conditions enabling line management enactment. This might also have to do with the increased application of integrated management in many organizations, because of which line managers consider it to be quite normal to carry out a range of activities, such as record-keeping, compliance, safety, and ... HRM.

4.   FRONT LINE MANAGERS AND PEOPLE MANAGEMENT

Purcell and Kinnie (2006) make a strong case for the important role of front-line managers (those having direct supervisory responsibility) with respect to the effectiveness of HR practices. In combination with general leadership capabilities, they are the ones linking intended and actual HR practices to the way in which these are being perceived by the employees. Line managers have a key role in shaping the employees' perception of HR practices (Purcell & Hutchinson, 2007). The concept of *people management*, as coined by Purcell and Hutchinson (2007), is meant to take into account the very combination of the role of line managers in implementing HR practices as well as their leadership behaviour which is crucial for the proper development of high-quality interpersonal relationships with their employees. Employees will be influenced by both and will react to it in a positive or negative way.

The empirical research as carried out by Purcell and Hutchinson (2007) confirms the symbiotic relationship between leadership behaviour and the enactment of HR practices. They are intrinsically interwoven and influence affective organizational commitment and positive job experiences. An explanation for this can be found, according to Purcell and Hutchinson (2007), in social exchange theory. Based on the proper implementation and application of HR practices in combination with the effective development of interpersonal relationships, the employees perceive organizational support (POS), which they reciprocate in the form of affective organization commitment, higher organizational citizenship behaviour (OCB), and better retention/attendance.

Building on the concept of people management, Knies and Leisink (2014) link the way in which employees perceive the people management activities of their line managers to the so-called AMO model in order to check its contribution to extra role behaviour. AMO is an acronym for Ability, Motivation and Opportunity. Both ability and motivation (operationalized as commitment) have a direct effect on extra role behaviour, where opportunity (operationalized as autonomy) has an indirect effect (through commitment) on extra role behaviour.

Big and Small AMO

The AMO model (see Chapter 4, this book) has been applied quite frequently to explain and validate High Performance work systems and their effect upon the performance of employees. In these cases, the AMO model is related to the ability, motivation, and opportunity of the employees/workers. However, it is also possible to use the AMO model to clarify and explain the effectiveness of line managers' HRM implementation. So, we have 'big' AMO applied to all the workers, and we have 'small' AMO, in which we only relate ability, motivation and opportunity of line managers towards their HRM, preferably said people management responsibilities. Carrying out a survey in two organizations among 174 line managers and more than 1,000 of their subordinates, Bos-Nehles et al. (2013), applying the model of small AMO, found out that ability is the best predictor of a line manager's HRM performance. This kind of performance has been measured in terms of employee satisfaction regarding the way their line manager carried out HRM activities in practice. Motivation of line managers for carrying out their HRM responsibilities did not matter, at least not in this empirical study. However, opportunity did enhance their ability. By opportunity in this respect, Bos-Nehles et al. (2013) refer 'to support from HR professionals, capacity to spend enough time on HRM tasks and clear and valuable policies and procedures' (2013, p. 866).

Strength of the HRM System

Finally, authors such as Purcell and Hutchinson (2007), Sanders and Frenkel (2011), and Knies and Leisink (2014) link the important role of people management as carried out by line managers to the creation of a strong HR situation (see Chapter 7 on HRM strength, this book). Dimensions such as *distinctiveness* imply that a set of HR practices 'stands out from the broader environment; that they are able to draw attention and will arouse interest' (Bowen & Ostroff, 2004, p. 208). For this to happen, the following four mechanisms are important: 'visibility of the HR practices, understandability of the HR practices, relevance of these practices for achieving both strategic as well as individual goals, and legitimacy/authority of the HR function' (Ostroff & Bowen, 2016, p. 197). Next to this important dimension, *consensus* between HR and line managers is important as is *consistent* implementation (Sanders & Frenkel, 2011). In this way a strong HR system combined with a visible line manager enacting people management can stimulate a strong relationship between HRM, climate, and performance (Knies & Leisink, 2014). Or, in the words of Purcell and Hutchinson, it is a way of 'communicating to employees the nature of the firm, their value to it and the type of behaviours expected' (2007, p. 7).

Figure 9.2 (Paauwe, Personal Communication, April 2019) highlights, by way of summary, all the factors that have been mentioned so far. It is important to realize that a line manager reflects on HR practices by looking through a specific lens, which depicts all the factors that play a role in whether or not they are able to carry out HRM activities in a proper way. Evaluating all these factors as summed up below will determine the degree of implementation by the line manager and how he or she assesses the added value of the HR function.

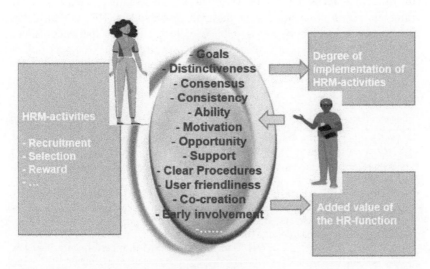

Figure 9.2   Strength of the HR situation

5.   IN CONCLUSION

Reflecting on the evolution of the relationship between HR and line management, we see an increase in the interaction between both parties as well as
other stakeholders such as employees, trade unions, shareholders, customers,
etc. Line management enactment is heading in the direction of co-creation.
Hewett and Shantz (2021, p. 2) define 'HR co-creation as a continuous process
in which HR and stakeholders create value through collaborative efforts to
problem-solve and innovate in the design and use of HR practices to help
them to better satisfy stakeholders' needs'. Hewett and Shantz (2021) indicate
three different but interlocked spheres, which help to clarify the process of
value creation through co-creation. The first one is the HR sphere, where HR
(often with the help of consultants) is involved in designing new HR practices
which might have potential value, for example a new onboarding program.
Whether such a practice really generates value depends on the users of it. The
second sphere is the user sphere, where we encounter users such as employees, managers at different hierarchical levels, trade union representatives,
etc. Independently from HR, they can also be involved in value creation for
example by selecting and adapting HR practices to make sure that these better
meet with their needs in a specific situation or department or job, for example
allowing for flexible working times. The third sphere is the joint one, where
HR and users are involved in co-design and collaborative use, in short where

the different stakeholders, inclusive of HR, are involved in co-creation. Apart from its role in co-creating with the main stakeholders, HR will fulfill an important role in this sphere as it is able to collect and share experiences across the different parts of the organization. In this way, it facilitates the diffusion of HR innovations across the organization (Hewett and Shantz, 2021).

REFERENCES

Bond, S., & Wise, S. (2003). Family leave policies and devolution to the line. *Personnel Review*, 32(1), 58–72. https://doi.org/10.1108/00483480310454727.

Bos-Nehles, A. C. (2010). *The Line Makes the Difference: Line Managers as Effective HR Partners.* (Doctoral dissertation, University of Twente). https://research.utwente.nl/files/6082386/thesis_A_Bos-Nehles.pdf.

Bos-Nehles, A. C., van Riemsdijk, M. J., & Looise, J. K. (2013). Employee perceptions of line management performance: Applying the AMO theory to explain the effectiveness of line managers' HRM implementation. *Human Resource Management*, 52(6), 861–877. https://doi.org/10.1002/hrm.21578.

Bowen, D. E., & Ostroff, C. (2004). Understanding HRM-firm performance linkages: The role of the "strength" of the HRM system. *Academy of Management Review*, 29(2), 203–221. https://doi.org/10.5465/amr.2004.12736076.

Guest, D. (1989). Personnel and HRM. *Personnel Management*, 21(1), 48–51.

Guest, D., & Bos-Nehles, A. (2013). HRM and performance: The role of effective implementation. In J. Paauwe, D.E. Guest, & P.M. Wright (eds), *HRM and Performance: Achievements and Challenges* (pp. 79–96). Hoboken, NJ: Wiley-Blackwell.

Harris, L. (2001). Rewarding employee performance: Line managers' values, beliefs and perspectives. *International Journal of Human Resource Management*, 12(7), 1182–1192. https://doi.org/10.1080/09585190110068386.

Hewett, R., & Shantz, A. (2021). A theory of HR co-creation. *Human Resource Management Review*, 31(4), 1–17. https://doi.org/10.1016/j.hrmr.2021.100823.

Knies, E., & Leisink, P. (2014). Linking people management and extra-role behaviour: Results of a longitudinal study. *Human Resource Management Journal*, 24(1), 57–76. https://doi.org/10.1111/1748-8583.12023.

Nishii, L. H., & Wright, P. (2008). Variability at multiple levels of analysis: Implications for strategic human resource management. In D. B. Smith (ed.), *The People Make the Place* (pp. 225–248). Mahwah, NJ: Erlbaum.

Ostroff, C., & Bowen, D. E. (2016). Reflections on the 2014 decade award: Is there strength in the construct of HR system strength? *Academy of Management Review*, 41(2), 196–214. https://doi.org/10.5465/amr.2015.0323.

Purcell, J., & Hutchinson, S. (2007). Front-line managers as agents in the HRM-performance causal chain: Theory, analysis and evidence. *Human Resource Management Journal*, 17(1), 3–20. https://doi.org/10.1111/j.1748-8583.2007.00022.x

Purcell, J., & Kinnie, N. (2006). HRM and business performance. In P. Boxall, J. Purcell, & P. Wright (eds), *The Oxford Handbook of Human Resource Management* (pp. 533–551). Oxford: Oxford University Press.

Renwick, D. (2003). Line manager involvement in HRM: An inside view. *Employee Relations*, 25(3), 262–280. https://doi.org/10.1108/01425450310475856.

Sanders, K., & Frenkel, S. (2011). HR-line management relations: Characteristics and effects. *International Journal of Human Resource Management*, 22(8), 1611–1617. https://doi.org/10.1080/09585192.2011.565644.

Wright, P. M., & Nishii, L. H. (2013). Strategic HRM and organizational behavior: Integrating multiple levels of analysis. In J. Paauwe, D.E. Guest & P.M. Wright (eds), *HRM & Performance: Achievements & Challenges*. Chichester: Wiley.

10. Job Demands Resources theory: how to stimulate engagement and to avoid burn-out?

TRIGGER

She had just graduated cum laude at the business school. Through her involvement as a student-assistant working for a professor who also happened to be active in consultancy for the business community, she got herself a challenging job working as an assistant-to for the Chief HR Officer (CHRO) of an innovative high-tech company. He was a hardworking man, stimulating for his subordinates, ambitious to get things done and challenging his co-workers. The assistant-to was drawn into this kind of work climate, adapted quickly, and managed to get all the challenges done, while also enjoying it immensely. Working hours did not matter so long as the job was done in time and completed at the required quality level. The CHRO reported to the professor that he was very happy with the recommendation to hire the graduate. After a year and a half, the professor met with the assistant-to during a conference. While talking to her he noticed that she was still very energetic and enthusiastic about the learning experiences within the company, yet she looked tired, with bags under her eyes and very pale looking. While travelling back, he wondered whether she was maybe a bit too engaged and that she might run the risk of suffering from a burnout in due course.

1.   MEANING OF THE CONCEPT AND HOW IT CAN HELP PRACTITIONERS

People working in organizations are faced with both demands and with resources. Demands such as pressing deadlines, too much work, and conflicting expectations can all lead to problems such as stress, anxiety, poor sleep, and might even end up in a long-lasting burnout. Resources such as social support, feedback on performance, appreciation, and enough autonomy for determining your own way and pace of working can help to boost motivation and to feel engaged at work. The presence of enough job resources can help to counteract (act as a buffer) the negative effects of too many job demands. The Job Demands Resources (JDR) theory explains the interaction between job demands and job resources and how that can result either in strain, stress, or burn-out, or in positive outcomes such as feeling motivated, engaged, etc. The JDR model can be applied to a wide range of job occupations in different sectors of the economy. The focus is on improving both performance and employee well-being. As such, the JDR model is an important tool for both HR managers as well as line managers.

2.   FOUNDING FATHERS/MOTHERS/STATUS/ RELEVANCE

The forerunners of the JDR model are Karasek (1979) with his Demand-Control Model, and Siegrist (1996) with the Effort-Reward Imbalance model, being two important job stress models. Some people also mention Hobfoll (1989) with his Conservation of Resources theory. All these models apparently acted as a source of inspiration for Demerouti and Bakker, who around the turn of the century started publishing on the JDR model.[1] Both together, as well as working with other researchers, they have built and developed the JDR model and tested it empirically in a wide range of settings and job occupations. In the last two decades, they have also extended it to include topics such as leadership and job crafting, next to more practical tools, which can be used online by practitioners.

Demerouti works as a full professor at Eindhoven University of Technology, Department of Industrial Engineering and Innovation Sciences and is chairing the Human Performance Management Group. Bakker is a full professor of Work and Organizational Psychology, chairing the research group Work and Organizational Psychology of the Institute of Psychology at Erasmus University Rotterdam, The Netherlands. He is also heading the Center of Excellence for Positive Organizational Psychology. From 2009 until 2013 he was president of the European Association of Work and Organizational Psychology.

The JDR has been applied in thousands of organizations and has inspired hundreds of empirical studies across the globe. As such, it has been recognized as one of the leading job stress models. For an overview and inventory of these studies we refer to the following meta-analyses: Bakker et al. (2014); Crawford et al. (2010); Halbesleben (2010); Nahrgang et al. (2011).

3.   CONTENT OF THE JDR MODEL

Jobs have different job characteristics, which can have a large impact upon the well-being of employees. Think in this respect of strain, stress, fatigue, time needed for recovery, but also on a more positive note satisfaction, engagement, thriving, etc., with subsequent effects for performance, both at an individual level as well as for those working in teams. According to Bakker and Demerouti (2007) these characteristics, which are very specific per job, can be classified into two general categories being job demands and job resources, leading up to an overarching model that can be applied to various occupational settings. *Job demands*, such as work pressure and having to face emotionally demanding situations, '... are the physical, psychological, social or organizational aspects of the job, that require sustained physical and/or psychological effort or skill' (Bakker & Demerouti, 2007, p. 312). *Job resources* on the other hand, such as coaching by your supervisor, autonomy, constructive feedback, career opportunities, refer to '... those physical, psychological, social or organizational aspects of the job that are either/or: functional in achieving work goals; reduce job demands and the associated physiological and psychological cost; stimulate personal growth, learning and development' (Bakker & Demerouti, 2007, p. 312).

Job resources are plentiful and can be found at the level of the organization as a whole (for example, career opportunities, training and development programs), the organization of work (degree of autonomy, opportunity for voice, participation), interpersonal relations (support from your supervisor, colleagues, team spirit) and at the level of the task (for example getting feedback, autonomy, variety in the kind of skills one needs to use). Next to job resources, we also have personal resources, such as optimism and self-efficacy as being part of your personality. According to Bakker and Demerouti (2017, p. 275) personal resources '... refer to the beliefs people hold regarding how much control they have over their environment. Individuals who are high in optimism and self-efficacy believe that good things will happen to them and that they are capable to handle unforeseen events'.

Dual Process

As depicted in Figure 10.1, the JDR model (Bakker & Demerouti, 2007, p. 313) gives rise to two different processes, one on the negative side and one on the positive side. To start with the negative one, the so-called health impairment process, which refers to an overload of job demands, or a poorly designed job, which will exhaust the employee and may lead to health problems, such as strain. If this lasts for a long time, the person might suffer from a burn-out and/or depression (Hankanen et al., 2008, based on three years of longitudinal research among 2,500 dentists).

On the positive side, we have a motivational process: job resources, as indicated above, function as the main predictors of engagement. More important is the fact that job resources can also buffer the impact of job demands on strain.

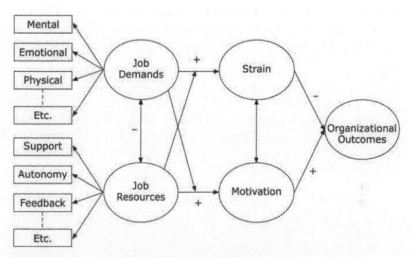

Note: Reprinted from 'The job demands-resources model: State of the art', by A. B. Bakker, and E. Demerouti, 2007, Journal of Management Psychology, 22(3), p. 313 (https://doi.org/10.1108/02683940710733315). Copyright 2007 by Emerald Group Publishing Limited.

Figure 10.1   The Job-Demands-Resources Model

If employees have sufficient access to job resources, it can help them to cope better with job demands. A good example in this respect is the study carried out by Xanthopoulou et al. (2007) among home care professionals. Job resources such as autonomy, social support, performance feedback, and opportunities for development were able to buffer the relationship between, on the one hand, job demands such as emotional demands, harassment by patients, high workload, etc. and on the other hand, burnout (Bakker & Demerouti, 2017, p. 274).

Bakker and Demerouti (2007, p. 315) sum up a range of examples of job resources (all backed up by empirical evidence) and why these can act as a buffer:

- A high quality relationship with one's supervisor: appreciation and support help to put the demands (work overload, physical demands) in another perspective.
- Job autonomy: this can add to employee health and well-being as greater autonomy allows to cope better with stressful situations.
- Social support: support from one's manager or colleagues (in whatever form) helps to ease, to attenuate the influence of work overload on strain.

- Constructive feedback: this will help employees to work more effectively. At the same time, it implies more positive communication between supervisors and employees.

One of the propositions of the JDR model is that job resources are especially important when job demands are high, which is the case when being involved in challenging jobs/activities, which require learning new skills, new behaviours. Research by Hankanen et al. (2005) confirmed this. When faced with job demands such as pupil misbehaviour, unfavourable physical work environment, job resources such as appreciation, innovativeness and skill variety were very conducive of work engagement.

4.   APPLICATIONS, USAGE, AND EMPIRICAL EVIDENCE

Below we highlight the further development of the JDR model, which due to its applications and thorough empirical testing can be considered as a tested theory.

JDR, Engagement and Burnout

More or less parallel with the development of the JDR model, the concept of engagement was developed by the research group at Utrecht University, headed by Schaufeli. The motivational process via job resources can stimulate engagement, also in situations with high job demands. Engagement refers to … 'a positive, fulfilling, work-related state of mind that is characterized by vigor, dedication and absorption' (Schaufeli & Bakker, 2004, p. 295). It is important to have a closer look at these three underlying dimensions, as they clarify how different engagement is compared to, for example, satisfaction or happiness. Somebody can be perfectly happy and satisfied at work, while reclining in his chair with folded arms, whereas engagement is not just a state of mind, but very often also visible in behaviour. Let us take a closer look, first at *vigour*, which is characterized 'by high levels of energy and mental resilience while working, the willingness to invest effort in one's work, and persistence also in the face of difficulties' (Schaufeli & Bakker, 2004, p. 295). The second element is *dedication*: 'A sense of significance, enthusiasm, inspiration, pride, and challenge' (Schaufeli & Bakker, 2004, p. 295). Finally, the third constituting element, which is *absorption*: 'being fully concentrated and happily engrossed in one's work, whereby time passes quickly, and one has difficulties with detaching oneself from work' (Schaufeli & Bakker, 2004, p. 295).

The other side of the coin is burnout, characterized by exhaustion (the opposite of vigour); by withdrawal, disengagement and cynicism (the opposite of dedication), and feelings of reduced personal accomplishment, sometimes also called reduced professional efficacy (Demerouti et al., 2001; Maslach et al., 1996).

Figure 10.2 (Schaufeli & Taris, 2014, p. 46) highlights the interaction between demands and resources, between strain and well-being, and how they result in outcomes, both positive (increased performance) and negative (health related problems).

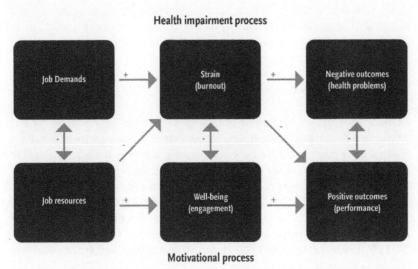

Health impairment process

Motivational process

Note: Reprinted from 'A critical review of the job demands-resources model: implications for improving work and health' by W. B. Schaufeli, and T. W. Taris. In Bridging Occupational, Organizational and Public Health (p. 46), by G. F. Bauer and O. Hämmig (eds), 2014, Springer Science + Business Media. Copyright 2014 by Springer Science + Business Media.

Figure 10.2   The revised job demands-resources (JD-R) model

Job Demands as Challenges or as Hindrances?

As the JDR model can be applied across a range of job occupations, there is no a priori definition or indication of the kind of job resources and job demands to be included. This is in contrast with the theories as developed by Karacek (1979) and Siegrist (1996), who both start from the premises of a pre-defined set of demands. In the JDR model, the specific job occupation specifies the resources and demands in that situation. Schaufeli and Taris (2014, p. 56) note that job demands are apparently negatively valued while job resources are positively valued. This once more emphasizes the *open* nature of the JDR model. In this respect, the meta-analysis by Crawford et al. (2010) is interesting. They distinguished two kinds of demands: *challenges* such as workload, time pressure, responsibility, and *hindrances* such as role conflict, role ambiguity, and red tape/bureaucracy (Schaufeli & Taris, 2014, p. 52; based on Crawford et al., 2010). Demands as challenges can have all kind of positive effects such as stimulating growth, mastery, learning, etc., whereas demands as hindrances could work out negatively in terms of blocking growth, learning, and achieving goals. The next step is to look at the consequences for engagement and then it appears (based on the meta-analysis carried out by Crawford et al., 2010) that hindrances relate negatively to engagement whereas challenges relate positively to engagement.

JDR and Leadership

Leaders/managers are very important for the creation of job resources for their employees. Research indicates that this is especially the case for transformational leadership as this style of leadership apparently increases the job resources for employees (Breevaart et al., 2014). In terms of specific behaviours, we can think of leaders displaying inspiration, having attention for the individual worker, and challenging the intellect of their followers (Bakker & Demerouti, 2017, p. 280). Subsequently this leads to job resources such as more autonomy, social support on a daily basis, participation in decision-making, etc. (see also Fernet et al., 2015). All these job resources help to cope with challenging job demands.

5.   JDR AND JOB CRAFTING

Instead of considering employees as only reacting to all kind of HRM and workplace interventions, we see nowadays more attention for the active, or even pro-active, role of employees themselves vis a vis creating their own working conditions and thus affecting themselves the kind of job demands they are facing and the supply of job resources being present. This has become known as job crafting. Tims et al. (2012) describe this as the proactive changes employees make in their job demands and resources. Wrzesniewski and Dutton (2001) are the original developers of this concept and distinguish task crafting (making pro-active changes in the work tasks of one's job), relationship crafting (the type/ nature of relationship engaged in at work), and cognitive crafting (what kind of meaning do we ascribe to our work). Think of a controller in an office with a long-standing service, who is getting increasingly more time due to automation and customized software, and uses this leeway in his work package for getting increasingly more involved in helping, coaching, mentoring newcomers in the company. Chapter 11 delves deeper into the topic of job crafting.

NOTES

1. The first full version of the JD-R model was published in the *Journal of Applied Psychology* (Demerouti, Bakker, Nachreiner, & Schaufeli, 2001) and was cited approximately more than 10,000 times in Google Scholar.

REFERENCES

Bakker, A. B., & Demerouti, E. (2007). The job demands-resources model: State of the art. *Journal of Management Psychology*, 22(3), 309–328. https://doi.org/10.1108/0268394071073315.

Bakker, A. B., & Demerouti, E. (2017). Job Demands-Resources Theory: Taking stock and looking forward. *Journal of Occupational Health Psychology*, 22(3), 273–285. http://dx.doi.org/10.1037/ocp0000056.

Bakker, A. B., Demerouti, E., & Sanz-Vergel, A. I. (2014). Burnout and work engagement: The JD-R approach. *Annual Review of Organizational Psychology and Organizational Behavior*, 1, 389–411. https://doi.org/10.1146/annurev-orgpsych-031413-09123.

Breevaart, K., Bakker, A. B., Hetland, J., Demerouti, E., Olsen, O. K., & Espevik, R. (2014). Daily transactional and transformational leadership and daily employee engagement. *Journal of Occupational and Organizational Psychology*, 87(1), 138–157. http://dx.doi.org/10.1111/joop.12041.

Crawford, E. R., LePine, J. A., & Rich, B. L. (2010). Linking job demands and resources to employee engagement and burnout: A theoretical extension and meta-analytic test. *Journal of Applied Psychology*, 95(5), 834–848. http://dx.doi.org/10.1037/a0019364.

Demerouti, E., Bakker, A. B., Nachreiner, F., & Schaufeli, W. B. (2001). The job demands-resources model of burnout. *Journal of Applied Psychology*, 86(3), 499–512.https://doi.org.10.1037/0021-9010.86.3.499.

Fernet, C., Trépanier, S., Austin, S., Gagné, M., & Forest, J. (2015). Transformational leadership and optimal functioning at work: On the mediating role of employees' perceived job characteristics and motivation. *Work & Stress: An International Journal of Work, Health & Organisations*, 29(1), 11–31. https://doi.org/10.1080/02678373.2014.1003998.

Hankanen, J., Bakker, A. B., & Demerouti, E. (2005). How dentists cope with their job demands and stay engaged: The moderating role of job resources. *European Journal of Oral Sciences*, 113(6), 479–487. https://doi.org/10.1111/j.1600-0722.2005.00250.x.

Hankanen, J. J., Schaufeli, W. B., & Ahola, K. (2008). The job demands resources model: A three-year cross-lagged study of burnout, depression, commitment, and work engagement. *Work & Stress*, 22(3), 224–241. https://doi.org/10.1080/02678370802379432.

Halbesleben, J. R. B. (2010). A meta-analysis of work engagement: Relationships with burnout, demands, resources and consequences. In A. B. Bakker, & M. P. Leiter (eds), *Work Engagement: A Handbook of Essential Theory and Research*. London: Psychology Press.

Hobfoll, S. E. (1989). Conservation of resources: A new approach at conceptualizing stress. *American Psychologist*, 44(3), 513–524. https://doi.org/10.1037/0003-066X.44.3.513.

Karasek, R. A. (1979). Job demands, job decision latitude and mental strain: Implications for job redesign. *Administrative Science Quarterly*, 24(2), 285–308. https://doi.org/10.2307/2392498.

Maslach, C., Jackson, S. E., & Leiter, M. P. (1996). *Maslach Burnout Inventory Manual* (3rd ed.). San Mateo, CA: Consulting Psychologists Press.

Nahrgang, J. D., Morgeson, F. P., & Hofmann, D. A. (2011). Safety at work: A meta-analytic investigation of the link between job demands and job resources, burnout, engagement, and   safety outcomes. *Journal of Applied Psychology*, 96(1), 71–94. https://doi.org/10.1037/a0021484.

Schaufeli, W. B., & Bakker, A. B. (2004). Job demands, job resources, and their relationship with burnout and engagement: A multi-sample study. *Journal of Organizational Behaviour*, 25(3), 293–315. https://doi.org/10.1002/job.248.

Schaufeli, W. B., & Taris, T. W. (2014). A critical review of the job demands-resources model: Implications for improving work and health. In G. F. Bauer & O. Hämmig (eds), *Bridging occupational, organizational and public health* (pp. 43-68). https:// doi.org/10.1007/978-94 -007-5640-3_4.

Siegrist, J. (1996). Adverse health effects of high-effort/low-reward conditions. *Journal of Occupational Health Psychology*, 1(1), 27–41. https://doi.org/10.1037/ 1076-8998.1.1.27.

Tims, M., Bakker, A. B., & Derks, D. (2012). Development and validation of the job crafting scale. *Journal of Vocational Behavior*, 80(1), 173–186. https://doi.org/10 .1016/j.jvb.2011.05.009.

Wrzesniewski, A., & Dutton, J. E. (2001). Crafting a job: Revisioning employees as active crafters of their work. *Academy of Management Review*, 26(2), 179–201. https://doi.org/10.5465/amr.2001.4378011.

Xanthopoulou, D., Bakker, A. B., Dollard, M. F., Demerouti, E., Schaufeli, W. B., Taris, T. W., & Schreurs, P. J. G. (2007). When do job demands particularly predict burnout? The moderating role of job resources. *Journal of Managerial Psychology*, 22(8), 766–786. https://doi.org/10.1108/02683940710837714.

11. Job design and crafting: how can we create an optimal work setting?

TRIGGER

An HR manager working in a big firm is known for her interests in quantitative data. Back home and among friends she is known for her computer and IT literacy. Being a graduate from Tilburg University, she is also trained in statistical methods for analysing data. In her present job, she thinks it a pity that the company is not doing a lot with the abundance of available data. In her leisure time she starts experimenting with combining data from the recently held engagement survey and linking it to financial and commercial performance data. It is a difficult job, because the data per business unit are not perfectly comparable, yet she manages to get some surprising and insightful relationships between leadership style and performance outcomes in certain departments and business-units. She decides to make a short presentation for the next Management Team meeting. Much to her surprise, her data driven insights are welcomed by her supervisor and colleagues, inclusive of the invitation to continue with that kind of analyses, but from now on during office hours.

1.   DEFINING THE CONCEPT AND ITS RELEVANCE FOR PRACTITIONERS

Job design or work design relates to 'the content and organization of one's work tasks, activities, relationships, and responsibilities' (Parker, 2014, p. 662). Job crafting as a related concept involves the shaping of jobs by employees themselves. Initially, job design involved a top-down approach, but based on experiments with work redesign, job enrichment and job rotation the redesign of jobs involves a variety of stakeholders, among which the employees themselves. This development has culminated in a more active and creating role of the employee him/herself, which recently has become known under the heading of job crafting.

Job design and crafting are important topics for a (HR) manager as the characteristics of a job in terms of variety, autonomy, etc. impact individual outcomes such as satisfaction, health, and well-being and at an organizational level, outcomes such as staff turnover and labour productivity.

2.   FOUNDING FATHERS/MOTHERS

Talking about job design, many people will refer to the famous Job Characteristics Model (JCM) of Hackman and Oldham (1975), which is prominently present in many study books on organization and management. However, the roots of the scientific study of job design date back a lot earlier. Think of Adam Smith (1776) discussing the benefits of simplification of jobs in order to speed up productivity, later on extended in the work by Taylor (1911). Under the heading of scientific management, he was advocating the idea of splitting up jobs into a narrow set of tasks, with minimal discretion on how to carry out the task. In this chapter we focus on the JCM of Hackman and Oldham, and the more recent add-on of job crafting, a concept which has become much in vogue since the publication of a paper on job crafting by Wrzesniewski and Dutton (2001) at the start of the new millennium.

The popularity of the JCM is overwhelming as well as the position of the two authors Hackman & Oldham who figure prominently at number eight on the list of 'heroes of employee engagement' (https://peakon.com/us/blog/tag/heroes-of-employee-engagement-us/) and whose names generate more than 38,000 hits in Google Scholar. As far as Wrzesniewski and Dutton are concerned, their paper has been cited almost 4,000 times since its publication in 2001.

3.   CONTENT OF THE THEORY: JOB DESIGN

Hackman and Oldham (1975, 1976) and Oldham and Hackman (2010) identified five key motivational job characteristics. These five subsequently impact an employee's sense of the meaning of work, his/her sense of responsibility, and his/her knowledge of the outcomes of the work activities.

Experienced meaningfulness, experienced responsibility, and knowledge of work outcomes are being labelled as critical psychological states, which either positively or negatively influence outcomes such as motivation, satisfaction, and work effectiveness. So, the starting point for the JCM are the five key motivational job characteristics:

- *Skill variety*: The degree to which a job requires different skills and activities in order to carry out the work. This implies that the worker needs to learn a variety of skills and develop his/her talents. Jobs become more *meaningful* if they require the use of a variety of skills and abilities.

- *Task identity*: The degree to which the job requires completion of a 'whole' and identifiable piece of work. Or in other words: doing a job from the beginning to the end with a visible outcome. Employees experience *more meaning* when they are involved in the whole process and are able to see the outcome of it instead of only a minor part.
- *Task significance*: The degree to which the job affects the life of others, either inside or outside the organization, in a meaningful way. If one's work has an impact upon others in terms of increasing their well-being, then the job becomes *more meaningful*.

NB the first three job characteristics impact mainly the psychological state of experienced meaningfulness.

- *Autonomy*: The degree to which the job provides substantial freedom, independence, and discretion to plan and carry out the work as well as determining yourself the procedures to be used in carrying out the job. The more this is the case, the greater the *experienced degree of personal responsibility* for your own successes and failures in the job.
- *Feedback*: The degree to which carrying out the work activities, required by the job, result in the employee getting direct and clear information about the effectiveness of his/her performance. If employees receive clear and adequate feedback, they will have better *knowledge of the results of their work*, which will also help them – if necessary – to improve their performance.

In the scheme below we depict the JCM with at, the heart of it, the three psychological states, which can be influenced (either positively or negatively) by the five key job characteristics. If positive then this will generate outcomes such as high motivation, a satisfied need for growth, job satisfaction and effectiveness in the job to the benefit of the organization as a whole.

Does the JCM work in every situation and for every worker? No, that is not the case, three so-called moderators (see Figure 11.1) impact on the relationships between job characteristics, psychological states, and outcomes:

- *Knowledge and skills*: For a job to be experienced as motivating, one needs to have the necessary knowledge and skills. If not, then it will discourage the different psychological states and subsequent outcomes.
- *Growth need strength*: People differ in the degree to which they are eager to learn and to develop themselves. This is expressed in the concept of Growth Need Strength, which is the strength of a person's need for development, learning, and achieving something (Oldham & Hackman, 2005).
- *Context satisfaction*: The setting of the job also impacts the kind of relationships and outcomes of the JCM. In this respect we can think of

contextual factors such as leadership, co-workers, pay, work climate, and job security. If the employee is satisfied with the context, then he/she can more optimally benefit from the motivating characteristics in the job itself. However, in case of dissatisfaction with the context, then the negative contextual factors will cost energy to handle, which will be at the expense of otherwise motivating characteristics of the job itself.

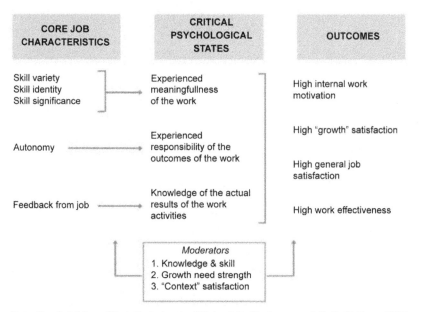

Note: Reprinted from Work Redesign (p. 90), by J. R. Hackman, and G. R. Oldham, 1980, Addison-Wesley. Copyright 1980 by Addison-Wesley.

Figure 11.1   Job characteristics model

4.   OUTCOMES AND EVIDENCE

Hackman and Oldham (1976), when presenting their model and underlying theory for the first time, provided at the same time the empirical data which they had collected to test the implications of their framework as depicted above. Their data (collected among 658 employees, working in 62 different jobs in seven organizations) confirmed the validity of their framework.

Their framework also triggered many other researchers to test it, which gave rise to a meta-analysis, carried out by Fried and Ferris (1987), which also supported the basic relationships within the model, albeit in a modest way. A more extensive meta-analysis, covering a wider variety of variables all relating to job design, was carried out by Humphrey et al. (2007). Their meta-analysis is based on 259 empirical studies, involving in total more than 200,000 participants. Next to the five motivational job characteristics as described above, Humphrey et al. (2007) also included social characteristics of the job (such as interdependence, feedback from others, social support, and interaction outside the organization) and work context characteristics (such as physical demands, work conditions, and ergonomics). As far as the variables included in the original JCM are concerned, they found rather strong support for the relationships between motivating job characteristics and outcomes such as job satisfaction, growth satisfaction, internal work motivation, and subjective job performance.

As far as the mediating role of the three psychological states was concerned, they found strong support for the role of experienced meaningfulness in relation to skill variety, task significance and task identity, and partial support for the mediating effect of experienced responsibility for autonomy. No support was found for the mediating effect of knowledge of results for feedback from the job (Humphrey et al., 2007, p. 1341).

Changes in the Workplace

The original framework was developed in a time when jobs were still well-described (job description) and related to a specific function. But since the 1970s, a lot has changed. The focus on shop floor workers and first line supervisors has shifted to line managers, professionals, and independent contract workers. Factory work has diminished in terms of number of workers employed due to mechanization and automatization. Jobs formerly involved in manual labour have disappeared, and/or upgraded to a higher level of carrying out programming, maintenance, and checking/controlling functions of the automated processes. The interdependence between workers has increased as well as working in teams, either real or virtual. So, interpersonal, social characteristics have become more important. That is also reflected in the meta-analysis by Humphrey et al. (2007) in which social/interactional characteristics also display strong relationships with satisfaction and subjective performance. Moreover, it will also give rise to other valued outcomes, such as altruistic behaviour, helping others, satisfaction with co-workers, and the cohesiveness of the unit or team, where the work is performed (Oldham & Hackman, 2010, p. 469). In combination with changes in the nature of work (more knowledge driven, more service orientated, more interpersonal, and more own responsibility for carrying out the work) employees face more autonomy, latitude in their work, not only for how to carry it out, but also for customizing, modifying, and crafting it. In this respect, Oldham & Hackman refer to the paper by Wrzesniewski and Dutton (2001) on job crafting which in no time drew a lot of attention and follow-up empirical research.

5.   CONTENT OF THE THEORY: JOB CRAFTING

Job crafting entails what employees themselves do to redesign their job in such a way that it can increase job satisfaction, engagement, resilience, and thriving at work (Wrzesniewski & Dutton, 2001). Job crafting can take place in several ways:

- *Crafting the nature and boundary of their tasks* by taking on more or fewer task (see the example at the start of this chapter), expanding or diminishing the scope of tasks or changing how tasks are being performed, for example by making use of advanced software or hardware.
- *Crafting their relationships at work* by changing the nature, frequency, or extent of their interactions with other people (think of the example of the administrator increasingly involved in socializing newcomers).
- *Crafting the way workers cognitively perceive and define their job and related tasks.* Berg, Dutton and, Wrzesniewski (2007) mention the example of the cleaner who redefines his work in a hospital from just cleaning to helping ill people.

The central characteristic of job crafting is that employees alter their tasks on their own initiative (Tims et al., 2012). It can happen without formal involvement or formally sanctioned by managers. However, based on the nature of job crafting it can impact both individual and organizational performance, either to the good or to the bad. Managers need to be prepared for the consequences and be aware how they can foster positive job crafting and avoid negative job crafting. The depth of job crafting is dependent upon the available degree of autonomy already present in the job. In the case of an assembly-line worker there is, for example, less autonomy and less discretion. Yet, job crafting is still possible. For example, in the Volvo Truck Assembly Plant in Zwolle (The Netherlands), every week one or two workers will be rewarded for an innovative idea. Very often this idea implies a change in work procedures, the use of equipment, tools, etc., so even in such a highly structured situation job crafting is possible.

6.   OUTCOMES OF JOB CRAFTING: EVIDENCE AND APPLICATION

The concept of job crafting is rather recent, and we cannot dispose of a large number of empirical papers testing the concept and its related outcomes. However, we can still safely conclude several positive outcomes (based on Demerouti & Bakker, 2014) such as commitment (Ghitulescu, 2007), readiness to change (Lyons, 2008), work engagement and in-role performance (Tims et al., 2012), and performance at work (Leana et al., 2009).

Based on these positive outcomes, it is recommendable for managers to create a context which fosters job crafting. The following steps are useful to consider as an approach towards beneficial job crafting. (Beneficial both for the well-being and engagement of the worker as well as for the organization towards achieving her goals.)

A stepwise approach to job-crafting (based on Berg et al., 2007, p. 7; theory to practice briefing):

- First step: Designing jobs that leave room for crafting. This implies designing jobs that have some leeway, some autonomy for changing tasks, relationships, or the cognitive meaning of it. However, a warning is also in place, job crafting is not always in the interest of the organization. It might benefit the well-being and engagement of the one who has 'job-crafted', but this might be at the expense of his/her colleagues or the new emphasis in the job is not in line with the overall goals of the organization. For this reason, the next step is just as well important to take into account.
- Second step: Creating and sustaining a work context that fosters 'beneficial' job crafting – beneficial to both the individual as well as the organization. How to do that? By building and communicating a shared understanding that job crafting is acceptable and can even be furthered as long as it is in line with organizational goals. Maintaining open lines of communication with the employees is important for a manager in order to avoid detrimental job crafting and to instead promote favourable crafting (Berg et al., 2007, p. 7).
- Third step: Building a climate of trust. Employees will probably be less resourceful and less creative in job crafting if they do not feel trusted. So, trusting relationships – especially with management – will help to unlock the potential for job crafting.

REFERENCES

Berg, J. M., Dutton, J. E., & Wrzesniewski, A. (2007). *What is Job Crafting and Why Does It Matter?* Ann Arbor MI: University of Michigan Ross School of Business. https://positiveorgs.bus.umich.edu/wp-content/uploads/What-is-Job-Crafting-and-Why-Does-it-Matter1.pdf.
Demerouti, E., & Bakker, A. B. (2014). Job crafting. In M. C. W. Peeters, J. de Jonge, & T. W. Taris (eds), *An Introduction to Contemporary Work Psychology* (pp. 414–433). Hoboken, NJ: Wiley Blackwell.
Fried, Y., & Ferris, G. R. (1987). The validity of the job characteristics model: A review and meta-analysis. *Personnel Psychology*, 40(2), 287–322. https://doi.org/10.1111/j.1744-6570.1987.tb00605.x.

Ghitulescu, B. E. (2007). *Shaping Tasks and Relationships at Work: Examining the Antecedents and Consequences of Employee Job Crafting* (Doctoral dissertation, University of Pittsburgh). http://d-scholarship.pitt.edu/10312/.

Hackman, J. R., & Oldham, G. R. (1975). Development of the job diagnostic survey. *Journal of Applied Psychology*, 60(2), 159–170. https://doi.org/10.1037/h0076546.

Hackman, J. R., & Oldham, G. R. (1976). Motivation through the design of work: Test of a theory. *Organizational Behavior and Human Performance*,16(2), 250–279. https://doi.org/10.1016/0030-5073(76)90016-7.

Hackman, J. R., & Oldham, G. R. (1980). *Work Redesign*. Boston: Addison Wesley.

Herzberg, F. (1966). *Work and the Nature of Man*. Cleveland: World.

Humphrey, S. E., Nahrgang, J. D., & Morgeson, F. P. (2007). Integrating motivational, social, and contextual work design features: A meta-analytic summary and theoretical extension of the work design literature. *Journal of Applied Psychology*, 92(5), 1332–1356. https://doi.org/10.1037/0021-9010.92.5.1332.

Leana, C., Appelbaum, E., & Shevchuk, I. (2009). Work process and quality of care in early childhood education: The role of job crafting. *Academy of Management Journal*, 52(6), 1169–1192. https://doi.org/10.5465/amj.2009.47084651.

Lyons, P. (2008). The crafting of jobs and individual differences. *Journal of Business Psychology*, 23(1–2), 25–36. https://doi.org/10.1007/s10869-008-9080-2.

Oldham, G. R., & Hackman, J. R. (2005). How job characteristics theory happened. In K. G. Smith, & M. A. Hitt (eds), *Great Minds in Management: The Process of Theory Development* (pp. 151–170). Oxford: Oxford University Press.

Oldham, G. R., & Hackman, J. R. (2010). Not what it was and not what it will be: The future of job design research. *Journal of Organizational Behavior*, 31(2–3), 463–479. https://doi.org/10.1002/job.678.

Parker, S. K. (2014). Beyond motivation: Job and work design for development, health, ambidexterity, and more. *Annual Review of Psychology*, 65, 661–691. https://doi.org/10.1146/annurev-psych-010213-115208.

Smith, A. (1776). *An Inquiry into the Nature and Causes of the Wealth of Nations*. W. Strahan & T. Cadell.

Taylor, F. W. (1911). *The Principles of Scientific Management*. New York: Harper & Brothers.

Tims, M., Bakker, A. B., & Derks, D. (2012). Development and validation of the job crafting scale. *Journal of Vocational Behavior*, 80(1), 173–186. https://doi.org/10.1016/j.jvb.2011.05.009.

Wrzesniewski, A., & Dutton, J. E. (2001). Crafting a job: Revisioning employees as active crafters of their work. *Academy of Management Review*, 26(2), 179–201. https://doi.org/10.5465/amr.2001.4378011.

12. Psychological contract theory: fulfillment or violation?

TRIGGER

Working like hell and not getting a bonus or a pay increase. That is what happened to Shaun when he was a management trainee in his first job after graduation. He did like the new job a lot. It was a combination of policy development, assisting in training programs, and acting as a moderator and secretary for the central works council. A lot of variety and a great learning experience. He did receive a lot of praise for the kind of work he was doing, so one can imagine that he was curious about the level of the 'end of year' bonus and his possible first salary increase. During the talk, his boss confirmed the outstanding quality and quantity of his work, yet for the next year, no bonuses and no pay increase would be given due to the dire economic circumstances. This decision had been taken at corporate level and no one would be entitled to any increase or bonus. Well, he did regret the outcome of the appraisal talk, yet based on the ongoing recession and being himself an economist, he could imagine that the company had opted for this decision. However, a few weeks later, he learned – through the grapevine – that the company had given a bonus and pay increase to their top managers, in spite of claiming that there would be no exception. From that moment onwards, he perceived an unfair balance between what he had contributed and what he got in return compared to others.

1. DEFINING THE CONCEPT AND HOW IT CAN HELP PRACTITIONERS

The employment relationship can be considered as an exchange relationship. The employee performs, brings ideas to the table, is collegial/amicable, has fun with his/her colleagues, develops himself and in return gets (monetary) rewards, appreciation, colleagues, opportunity for development, etc. To a certain degree this is also laid down in a formal written labour contract, which is also having a legal status. However, not everything can be covered by a formal labour contract. The parties involved also have their perceptions of the kind of reciprocal promises and obligations in that relationship. Parties might differ to what degree these promises are being delivered (*fulfillment* of the psychological contract) or to what degree the implicit promises have been *broken* or violated, with all kinds of negative consequences both for the employee and for the organization.

From a line manager's and/or HR perspective, it is important to be aware of this, as the degree of fulfillment or violation impacts on the motivation, performance, and well-being of the employees, as well as on their intention to stay or to leave the company. So, careful communication about implicit promises and obligations is important, as well as having a continuous dialogue with employees based on trust and mutual respect. HRM practices such as fairness/equity in rewards, opportunities for career and development can help towards fulfilling the psychological contract, which will result in outcomes such as commitment, job satisfaction, and increased job performance.

2. FOUNDING FATHERS/MOTHERS

The origins of the psychological contract date back to the 1960s (Argyris, 1960; Levinson, 1962) in order to indicate the subjective nature of the employment relationship. Also, more general theories such as social exchange theory (Blau, 1964), equity theory (Adams, 1965), and Gouldner (1960) with his norm of 'reciprocity' stimulated this kind of thinking. A more specific contribution was made by Schein (1965), who indicated that the psychological contract consists of a set of unwritten expectations operating continuously between every member of the organization and the various managers in that organization.

The concept became truly established the very moment Rousseau (1989) became active in this area – not only conceptually, but also fulfilling an important role in carrying out and stimulating empirical research for the next two decades. In the end, working together with other people created a community of researchers involved in testing and extending the concept of the psychological contract. In this respect we refer to Robinson, Morrisson, Conway, Coyle-Shapiro, Kessler, and of course, Guest. With the latter, Rousseau had an on-going debate about their different ways of defining the psychological contract and the value of it as a theoretical construct (or not). In the Netherlands, academics such as Schalk (see amongst others, Anderson & Schalk, 1998), Freese (Freese et al., 2011), and Bal (see later on) have been active in this area. Nowadays, all the conceptual and empirical work has led to an established theory, well-tested as evidenced in meta-analyses. In this respect, we mention Zhao et al. (2007) and Bal et al. (2008). Just to give an indication of the popularity of the concept: in December 2023 typing 'psychological contract' into Google generated more than 140 million hits. For Google Scholar, the number of hits is 2,600,000. Rousseau herself, albeit not the founding mother, is the most prominent scholar in this area. Her book, *Psychological Contracts in Organizations* (1995), has been cited more than 9,000 times (Google Scholar, December 2023). She has been a president of the Academy of Management (AoM) and in 2009 she received the Lifetime Career Achievement Award of the AoM.

3. CONTENT OF THE THEORY

Key words in defining the concept of the psychological contract are perception or belief. See, for example, Argyris (1960), who defined it as the perception of both parties to the employment relationship, organization and individual, of the obligations implied in the relationship. Later on, Rousseau (1989) defines it as an individual's belief regarding the terms and conditions of the reciprocal exchange agreement between the focal person and another party. A psychological contract emerges when one party believes that a *promise* of future return has been made, a contribution has been given and thus, an *obligation* has been created to provide future benefits. So it is all about perceived promises and obligations, mutuality and whether promises have been met or not.[1] Bear in mind that it is not about the *fact* of mutuality but about the *perception* of mutuality by an organizational member.

Breach, Fulfillment, and Violation

What happens when perceived promises have not been met? We call this a breach of the psychological contract, which is the employee's perception regarding the extent to which the organization has failed to fulfill its promises or obligations (Robinson & Rousseau, 1994). The opposite of breach is fulfillment, which is the perception (NB again, perception!) of an employee that his employer has fulfilled the promised obligations of the psychological contract. According to Robinson and Rousseau (1994), contract breach is not so much an exception but more the norm, as they found that the majority of their respondents reported that reciprocal obligations had been breached. Coyle-Shapiro and Kessler (2000) also found the majority of their respondents to have experienced contract breach. Guest (1998) notes that this kind of frequency of breach might also have to do with the unwritten and unspoken promises and obligations as perceived by the employee. So how can an organization ever meet these expectations? Moreover, who or what is acting as an agent on behalf of the organization? Is it top management, your direct supervisor, etc.?

When *breach* is experienced as being severe or frequently taking place, it can easily lead to *violation* of the psychological contract. The difference between the two is as follows: 'Perceived breach refers to the cognition that one's organization has failed to meet one or more obligations within one's psychological contract in a manner commensurate with one's contribution' (Morrison & Robinson, 1997, p. 230). Violation is defined as 'an affective and emotional experience of disappointment, frustration, anger, and resentment that may emanate from an employee's interpretation of a contract breach and its accompanying circumstances' (Morrison & Robinson, 1997, p. 242).

Effects and the Importance of Trust

In case of fulfillment of the psychological contract, one can expect to have positive employee outcomes, such as in-role performance, organizational citizenship behaviour (OCB),[2] job satisfaction, commitment and lower intentions to leave the company, whereas breach and violation will probably have the opposite and thus negative outcomes. Below (see section on empirical evidence) we report on the outcomes of meta-analytical studies. A number of studies also mention the importance of trust. Robinson and Rousseau (1994), and Robinson (1996) indicate that trust apparently functions as a mediator between, on the one hand, psychological contract breach and on the other hand, employee outcomes. Breach leads to a decrease in trust. Subsequently, the decrease in trust leads to a decrease in performance and OCB as well as an increase in turnover intentions. The importance of trust is later on confirmed in other studies. Deery et al. (2006) find that breach is related to lower organizational trust. The two meta-analytical studies by Zhao et al. (2007) and the one by Bal et al. (2008) also find that the more psychological contracts are breached, the lower the level of trust.

4.   EMBEDDING THE PSYCHOLOGICAL CONTRACT IN THE EMPLOYMENT RELATIONSHIP

Putting the psychological contract into the perspective of the two most important parties involved (i.e. employee and employer), the employee needs to pose two questions (Guest et al., 1996): What can I reasonably expect from the organization and what should I reasonably be expected to contribute in return? The first question will probably emphasize the following topics (Armstrong, 2010, Chapter 16):

- How am I treated in terms of fairness, equity, and consistency?
- Is there security of employment?
- Can I demonstrate/use my competency?
- What are the career expectations and opportunities for developing my skills?

- Is there enough opportunity for involvement and influence?
- Can I trust management of the organization to stick to their promises?

As far as the employer's perspective is concerned, the psychological contract would need to cover: competence, effort, compliance, commitment, and loyalty from the side of the employee (Armstrong, 2010, Chapter 16). This summing up of topics is also dependent on sector, educational level, situation on the labour market, etc. Therefore, it is important to frame the psychological contract not only in the employment relationship but also in the context of the specific organization, sector, country, and era. After all, the nature of the employment contract is subject to change. Nowadays, in many countries, there is less security, the variety in labour contracts has increased, and next to the employment relationship in its traditional sense a whole new (global) world of relations between demand and supply has emerged through the so-called 'gig' economy.

Below we depict the framework (see Figure 12.1) as developed by Guest (2004), which gives a good overview of contextual factors both at the individual and organizational levels, the kind of HRM policies and practices in place which subsequently impact on the psychological contract, and which lead to a certain 'state' of the psychological contract. 'State' indicates whether or not the promises and obligations have been met, whether they are fair, and their implications for trust (Guest, 2004; Guest & Conway, 2002). Again, we see the mediating role of trust and how this impacts employee outcomes (attitudinal and behavioural).

5.   EMPIRICAL EVIDENCE/RESULTS

The empirical evidence about the usefulness and applicability of the psychological contract theory is abundantly present. For the sake of convenience, we rely first of all on three meta-analyses. The first one is by Wanous et al. (1992) encompassing 31 studies. With a special focus on meeting the expectations of newcomers, they find reasonably strong positive effects for job satisfaction and organizational commitment. The second is by Zhao et al. (2007), whose meta-analysis is based upon 51 studies. Focusing on contract breach, they find a negative relationship with outcomes such as trust, organizational commitment, job satisfaction, OCB and in-role performance, and a positive relationship with turnover intentions. The latter indicates the greater the breach, the more employees are inclined to leave the organization. Zhao et al. (2007) also conclude that violation of a relational contract has as stronger negative impact on employee attitude and behaviour than violation of a transactional contract. Just like Zhao et al. (2007), the meta-analysis by Bal et al. (2008), based on

60 studies, finds that breach of the psychological contract relates negatively to organizational commitment and job satisfaction.

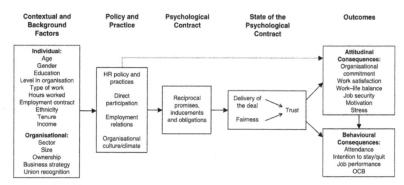

Note: Reprinted from 'The psychology of the employment relationship: An analysis based on the psychological contract', by D. Guest, 2004, Applied Psychology: An International Review, 53(4), p. 550 (https://doi.org/10.1111/j.1464-0597.2004.00187.x). Copyright 2004 by International Association for Applied Psychology.

Figure 12.1   A framework for applying the psychological contract to the employment relationship

Role of Age

As far as age is concerned, which is prominently included in the meta-analysis by Bal et al. (2008), they report the following: in case of breach of the psychological contract they expect that older people are better in regulating their emotions, so they will also react less emotionally to breach of the psychological contract. In their meta-analysis, this is indeed confirmed, but only with respect to organizational commitment. Younger people tend to react more strongly (in a negative way) towards breach of the contract than older people. Yet, this did not appear to be the case for job satisfaction – in this scenario, older people tended to react more negatively. An explanation, according to Bal et al. (2008), might be that older workers see or have less perspective for a job transfer to another company than their younger counterparts. Younger workers might – in case of breach of the contract – be inclined to lose their trust in the employer and will therefore be less committed to the organization, while still enjoying their work and thus reacting less strongly as far as job satisfaction is concerned.

IN CONCLUSION

The psychological contract is present in every employment relationship and determines to a large degree both performance and well-being in the exchange relationship between employee and employer. Violation or breach can be very disruptive for motivation and the quality of the interaction between employee and his or her manager/employer. We better make sure to pay attention to it in shaping the employment relationship. If done properly, fulfillment is within reach with all the positive effects, such as commitment, performance and well-being, attached to it.

NOTES

1. The attentive reader will have noticed that Argyris defines it as involving the perception of two parties, whereas in Rousseau's definition it is purely from the perception of one individual. This has given rise to a controversy between Rousseau and Guest (Guest (1998), Rousseau (1998) and again Guest (1998)), for which the *Journal of Organizational Behaviour* offered a platform in 1998. Enjoyable and useful reading for those who want to dig deeper.
2. Organ (1988) defines Organizational Citizenship Behaviour (OCB) as 'individual behavior that is discretionary, not directly or explicitly recognized by the formal reward system, and that in the aggregate promotes the effective functioning of the organization'. It is very much similar to the concept of extra role behaviour (ERB) defined as 'behavior that attempts to benefit the organization and that goes beyond existing role expectations' (Organ et al., 2006, p. 33).

REFERENCES

Adams, J. S. (1965). Inequity in social exchange. *Advances in Experimental Social Psychology*, 2, 267–299. https://doi.org/10.1016/S0065-2601(08)60108-2.

Anderson, N., & Schalk, R. (1998). The psychological contract in retrospect and prospect. *Journal of Organizational Behavior*, 19, 637–647. https://www.jstor.org/stable/3100280.

Argyris, C. (1960). *Understanding Organisational Behaviour*. California: Dorsey.

Armstrong, M. (2010). *Armstrong's Essential Human Resource Management Practice: A Guide to People Management*. London: Kogan Page Publishers.

Bal, P. M., De Lange, A. H., Jansen, P. G. W., & Van Der Velde, M. E. G. (2008). Psychological contract breach and job attitudes: A meta-analysis of age as a moderato. *Journal of Vocational Behavior*, 72(1), 143–158. https://doi.org/10.1016/j.jvb.2007.10.005.

Blau, P. (1964). *Exchange and Power in Social Life*. New York: Wiley.

Coyle-Shapiro, J. A. M., & Kessler, I. (2000). Consequences of the psychological contract for the employment relationship: A large scale survey. *Journal of Management Studies*, 37(1), 903–930. https://doi.org/10.1111/1467-6486.00210.

Deery, S. J., Iverson, R. D., & Walsh, J. T. (2006). Toward a better understanding of psychological contract breach: A study of customer service employees. *Journal of Applied Psychology*, 91(1), 166–175. https://doi.org/10.1037/0021-9010.91.1.166.

Freese, C., Schalk, R., & Croon, M. (2011). The impact of organizational changes on psychological contracts. *Personnel Review*, 40(4), 404–422. https://doi.org/10.1108/00483481111133318.

Gouldner, A. W. (1960). The norm of reciprocity: A preliminary statement. *American Sociological Review*, 25(2), 161–178. https://doi.org/10.2307/2092623.

Guest, D. E. (1998). Is the psychological contract worth taking seriously? *Journal of Organizational Behavior*, 19, 649–664. https:// doi .org/ 10 .1002/ (SICI)1099 -1379(1998)19:1+%3C649::AID-JOB970%3E3.0.CO;2-T.

Guest, D. E. (2004). The psychology of the employment relationship: An analysis based on the psychological contract. *Applied Psychology: An International Review*, 53(4), 541–555. https://doi.org/10.1111/j.1464-0597.2004.00187.x.

Guest, D. E., & Conway, N. (2002). *Organisational Change and the Psychological Contract.* Chartered Institute of Personnel and Development.

Guest, D. E., Conway, N., Briner, R., & Dickman, M. (1996). *The State of the Psychological Contract in Employment* (IPD Report No. 16). Institute of Personnel Development.

Levinson, H. (1962). *Organizational Diagnosis*. Cambridge, MA: Harvard University Press.

Morrison, E. W., & Robinson, S. L. (1997). When employees feel betrayed: A model of how psychological contract violation develops. *Academy of Management Review*, 22(1), 226–256. https://doi.org/10.5465/amr.1997.9707180265.

Organ, D. W. (1988). *Organizational Citizenship Behavior*. Lanham, MD: Lexington Books.

Organ, D. W., Podsakoff, P. M., & MacKenzie, S. B. (2006). *Organizational Citizenship Behavior: Its Nature, Antecedents, and Consequences.* London: SAGE.

Robinson, S. L. (1996). Trust and breach of the psychological contract. *Administrative Science Quarterly*, 41(4), 574–599. https://doi.org/10.2307/2393868.

Robinson, S. L., & Rousseau, D. M. (1994). Violating the psychological contract: Not the exception but the norm. *Journal of Organizational Behavior*, 15(3), 245–259. https://doi.org/10.1002/job.4030150306.

Rousseau, D. M. (1989). Psychological and implied contracts in organizations. *Employee Responsibilities and Rights Journal*, 2(2), 121–139. https:// doi .org/ 10 .1007/BF01384942.

Rousseau, D. M. (1998). The 'problem' of the psychological contract considered. *Journal of Organizational Behavior*, 19, 665–671. https:// www .jstor .org/ stable/ 3100282.

Schein, E. H. (1965). *Organizational Psychology*. Hoboken, NJ: Prentice Hall.

Wanous, J. P., Poland, T. D., Premack, S. L., & Davis, K. S. (1992). The effects of met expectations on newcomer attitudes and behaviors: A review and meta-analysis. *Journal of Applied Psychology*, 77(3), 288–297. https://doi.org/10.1037/0021-9010 .77.3.288.

Zhao, H., Wayne, S. J., Glibkowski, B. C., & Bravo, J. (2007). The impact of psychological contract breach on work-related outcomes: A meta-analysis. *Personnel Psychology*, 60(30), 647–680. https://doi.org/10.1111/j.1744-6570.2007.00087.x.

13. Psychological safety: the secret behind well-performing teams[1]

TRIGGER: *GOOGLE PROJECT ARISTOTLE*

A company that is renowned for collecting a lot of data about its employees is Google. In 2012, Google started a project in order to find out why some teams did very well and others not so well. To discover the secret behind the very well performing teams. Nowadays this is a very relevant topic as increasingly companies across the globe are emphasizing team work to deal with fast-paced change and knowledge-intensive work that cannot be captured anymore by individuals. Connectivity, agile working, and scrum approach are the new buzzwords in relationship to teamwork. According to Cross, Rebele, and Grant (2016), the time spent by managers and employees on collaborative activities has increased by 50% or more in the last two decades. However, all that time spent on collaborative activities can also become a burden, this is especially the case if a group or team is not working effectively and time is wasted on meetings without making any progress. So, one can easily understand the relevance of the research project initiated by Google (entitled Aristotle) to unravel the secret of well-performing teams.

The initial search was based on tracking data on comparable characteristics such as educational background, level, socializing out of work or not, same hobbies, being all introvert or extravert, gender balance, frequency, length of team membership, etc. However, in spite of Google being good at detecting patterns in data, teams with the same pattern still had very different levels of effectiveness. In the end they started to look for group norms. What are the habits, traditions, behavioural style, and unwritten rules, which regulate how we conduct our meetings? The research team discovered that in well-performing teams there was the opportunity for everybody to speak up and express his or her opinion (conversational turn-taking). Moreover, the members of the successfully operating teams also displayed a higher level of empathy, meaning that they were good at intuitively sensing how others felt based on their tone of voice, facial expression, body language, etc. In the end, all the pieces of the puzzle came together for the Google research team under the heading of psychological safety as being 'a sense of confidence that

*the team ... will not embarrass, reject of punish somebody for speaking up.
It describes a team climate characterized by interpersonal trust and mutual
respect in which people are comfortable being themselves' (Edmondson,
1999).*[2]

1.   DEFINING THE CONCEPT AND ITS RELEVANCE FOR PRACTITIONERS

Psychological safety is a shared belief that the team is safe for interpersonal
risk taking. It can be defined as 'being able to show and employ oneself
without fear of negative consequences of self-image, status or career' (Kahn,
1990, p. 708). As working within teams is increasing in organizations, it is
important to safeguard the right conditions for working together in an effective
and pleasant way. The most important concept in that respect is 'psychological
safety' as it contributes to teams being more innovative, having a higher performance, and being able to speed up learning within the team. In case a sufficient level of psychological safety is present, team members dare to learn from
mistakes and are more active in speaking up behaviour.

2.   FOUNDING FATHERS/MOTHERS

No doubt the founding mother of psychological safety is the Harvard Business
School professor Amy Edmondson, who wrote a thorough paper on the
topic which was published in 1999 in the top journal, *Administrative Science
Quarterly*. Since then, it has been cited more than 13,000 times. However,
there are some precursors to Edmondson. In 1990, Kahn defined it as follows:
'being able to show and employ oneself without fear of negative consequences
of self-image, status or career' (Kahn, 1990, p. 708). He was able to link
psychological safety as an enabler to personal engagement at work and emphasized the importance of group relationships based on trust and respect. Back
in the 1960s, people like Schein and Bennis (1965) had already concluded
that psychological safety is crucial for people to feel secure and capable of
changing their behaviour when confronted with organizational change and
challenges. Yet, the work by Edmondson caused a rejuvenation of empirical
research in this area and enables us to be quite conclusive about the factors that
contribute to it and the subsequent kind of outcomes, implications for individuals, teams, and organizations.

3.   CONTENT OF THE THEORY AND EVIDENCE

The focus of Edmondson's theory is on the functioning of teams and how the
presence of a sufficient degree of psychological safety will be beneficial for

learning and performance in organizational work teams. If people are working in a psychologically safe work environment, they will easily voice ideas, be open to feedback, give honest feedback themselves and be willing to collaborate, take risks and dare to experiment (Edmondson, 1999). Since her original conception and thoroughly testing this idea (including the development of a very reliable seven-items scale for measuring it), psychological safety has been tested by many others at different levels of analysis. Below we describe the factors (antecedents) that contribute to psychological safety at the individual/team level and the organizational level, and the kind of outcomes associated with it, all based on the systematic review, encompassing 78 studies, by Newman et al. (2017).

- *Supportive leadership behaviours* such as leader inclusiveness, offering support, being trustworthy, openness, and behavioural integrity all contribute to the perception of psychological safety, which in turn generates employee outcomes such as voice behaviours, involvement in creative work, job performance, and engagement (Newman et al., 2017, p. 525). Also, leadership styles such as transformational leadership, ethical leadership and shared leadership help to build psychological safety, which subsequently leads to outcomes such as employee voice, team learning, and individual learning.
- *Supportive organizational practices* such as employees' perceptions of organizational support, access to mentoring, and diversity practices strengthen the perception of psychological safety, which in turn increases organizational commitment and job performance (Newman et al., 2017, p. 525).
- *Outcomes of psychological safety (individual/team level)*: initially the focus was on learning and performance outcomes, yet with the increase in empirical studies since the 1999 publication of Edmondson, other outcomes have also been reported. Outcomes such as a greater reporting of treatment errors, more interpersonal communication (see among others Alingh et al., 2018; Leroy et al., 2012), and better knowledge sharing among team members (Newman et al., 2017, p. 526). Also interesting is the finding by Tynan (2005), that individuals who believe that others feel safe in their relationships (so-called other psychological safety) are more likely to raise disagreement, give candid feedback, and point out errors to their supervisor (Newman et al., 2017, p. 526).
- *Outcomes of psychological safety (organizational level):* research by Baer and Frese (2003) established that collective perceptions of psychological safety were strongly related to firm performance in terms of returns on assets and goal achievement. Other researchers established a link between employee perceptions of psychological safety and creativity (Carmeli et

al., 2010), creative thinking, and risk-taking (Palanski & Vogelsang, 2011), as well as innovation in R&D teams (Gu et al., 2013) and manufacturing process innovation performance (Lee et al., 2011).

In conclusion, the evidence concerning the beneficial effects at the individual, team, and organizational levels is overwhelming. Psychological safety is a very important concept, worthwhile to pursue in organizations. Below, Figure 13.1 depicts the model as developed by Newman et al. (2017, p. 530) to summarize the relationships as described in this section:

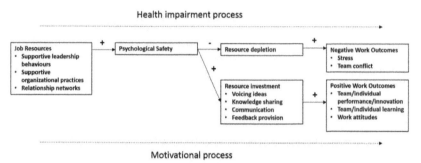

Note: Reprinted from 'Psychological safety: A systematic review of the literature', by A. Newman, R. Donohue, and N. Eva, 2017, Human Resource Management Review, 27(3), p. 530 (http://dx.doi.org/10.1016/j.hrmr.2017.01.001). Copyright 2017 by Elsevier.

Figure 13.1   An integrative framework of psychological safety

The starting point are job resources, such as supportive leadership style and high-quality relationships, which contribute to psychological safety. This will help to prevent the loss of job resources. If this is not the case, resource depletion will result in negative work outcomes such as, for example, stress and team conflicts (the so-called health impairment process). However, if we have a sufficient degree of psychological safety, then the members of such a team are also motivated to invest in additional resources such as knowledge-sharing, voicing ideas, giving feedback, etc. This will, in turn, lead to positive work outcomes such as learning, innovation, and performance. Instead of a health impairment process, we then have an increasingly stronger motivation in the team (motivational process) (Newman et al., 2017, p. 530).

4. APPLICATIONS AND RECOMMENDATIONS FOR MANAGERS: HOW TO MAKE IT WORK?

Based on the outcomes as described, we can be sure that psychological safety is an important characteristic of individuals, teams, and organizations, worthwhile to aim at. However, it does not emerge naturally, especially not when the work is uncertain and complex. Having the feeling of being at risk when giving suggestions is a severe barrier towards effective collaboration in teams (Edmondson & Lei, 2014). The degree of feeling safe or not in a group can, to a large extent, be attributed to the behaviour of managers and supervisors. They send out signals (either positive or negative) which impact on the willingness to take interpersonal risk, when giving input, suggestions, feedback, raising issues, offering contradicting views, etc. In this respect it is important for managers to take that into account and to see to it that their communications are congruent, help to build a climate for psychological safety, and show appreciation for employees who engage in such behaviours.

By way of illustrating what is at stake, we list the items as developed by Edmondson to measure[3] among respondents the degree to which they perceive psychological safety (NB reversed items (R) are also included):

- If you make a mistake on this team, it is often held against you (R).
- Members of this team are able to bring up problems and tough issues.
- People on this team sometimes reject others for being different (R).
- It is safe to take risks on this team.
- It is difficult to ask other members of this team for help (R).
- No one in this team would deliberately act in a way that undermines my efforts.
- Working with members of this team, my unique skills and talents are valued and utilized.

Returning back to the 'trigger' in the opening section of this chapter, we highlight the steps (based on an article by Laura Delizonna (2017, pp. 1–5)) as taken by Google's head of industry Paul Santagata to increase the psychological safety of its team:

1. *'Approach conflict as a collaborator, not an adversary*. Handle conflict with a collaborative attitude by seeking a mutually desirable solution. Avoid triggering a fight or flight reaction, true success is a win-win outcome' (Delizonna, 2017, p. 3).
2. *'Speak human to human.* Everyone has similar objectives and needs that must be recognised, such as that one wants to feel respected, appreciated,

and competent, just like you yourself. Behaving in this way will promote trust and positive behaviour' (Delizonna, 2017, p. 3).

3. *'Anticipate reactions and plan countermoves.* When you need to communicate something, prepare for the most likely reactions, and how one should respond to each possible reaction. Quoting Paul Santagata: "Looking at the discussion from this third-party perspective exposes weaknesses in my positions and encourages me to rethink my argument". More specifically, he asks, "What are my main points? What are the three ways my listeners are most likely to react? Finally, how will I respond to each of those scenarios?"' (Delizonna, 2017, pp. 3–4).

4. *'Replace blame with curiosity.* The very moment you are trying to blame team members, they will become defensive, less open, and less engaged. Being curious is the alternative, take on a learning mode, signal the problem, ask for possible causes, background information, and engage the group in a conversation in order to explore causes and find possible solutions' (Delizonna, 2017, p. 4).

5. *'Ask for feedback on delivery.* Asking for feedback illuminates black spots in your way of communicating. It models fallibility, vulnerability, demonstrates openness to learning, which all increase trust' (Delizonna, 2017, p. 4).

6. *'Measure psychological safety.* Ask your employees how safe they feel and how they think their feelings of safety can be increased. Use the item list as indicated above. Do it on a regular basis and discuss outcomes' (Delizonna, 2017, p. 5).

Next to offering support, being open, available, and responsive to input by team members, it will also help if leaders/managers provide clear direction, have an appealing vision, and are able to frame a strategy in an inspiring way, inclusive of clearly stated goals. This will stimulate learning, development opportunities, and performance.

NOTES

1. This chapter has made extensive use of the overview paper by Edmonson and Lei, entitled: Psychological safety: The history, renaissance and future of an interpersonal construct as published in the *Annual Review of Organizational Psychology and Organizational Behavior*, 2014.
2. Excerpt from *New York Times* article by Charles Duhigg (2016), summarized by author.
3. Seven-point scale from 'very inaccurate' to 'very accurate'.

REFERENCES

Alingh, C. W., van Wijngaarden, J. D. H., van de Voorde, K., Paauwe, J., & Huijsman, R. (2018). Speaking up about patient safety concerns: The influence of safety management approaches and climate on nurses' willingness to speak up. *BMJ Quality & Safety*, 28(1), 39–48. https://doi.org/10.1136/bmjqs-2017-007163.

Baer, M., & Frese, M. (2003). Innovation is not enough: Climates for initiative and psychological safety, process innovations, and firm performance. *Journal of Organizational Behaviour*, 24(1), 45–68. https://doi.org/10.1002/job.179.

Carmeli, A., Reiter-Palmon, R., & Ziv, E. (2010). Inclusive leadership and employee involvement in creative tasks in the workplace: The mediating role of psychological safety. *Creativity Research Journal*, 22(3), 250–260. https://doi.org/10.1080/10400419.2010.504654.

Cross, R., Rebele, R., & Grant, A. (2016). Collaborative overload. *Harvard Business Review*, 94(1), 74–79. https://hbr.org/2016/01/collaborative-overload.

Delizonna, L. (2017). High performing teams need psychological safety. Here's how to create it. *Harvard Business Review*, 8, 1–5. https://hbr.org/2017/08/high-performing-teams-need-psychological-safety-heres-how-to-create-it.

Duhigg, C. (2016, February 25). What Google learned from its quest to build the perfect team. *The New York Times Magazine*. https://www.nytimes.com/2016/02/28/magazine/what-google-learned-from-its-quest-to-build-the-perfect-team.html?_r=0&referer=http://lnkd.in.

Edmondson, A. (1999). Psychological safety and learning behavior in work teams. *Administrative Science Quarterly*, 44(2), 350–383. https:// doi .org/ 10 .2307 %2F2666999.

Edmondson, A. C., & Lei, Z. (2014). Psychological safety: The history, renaissance, and future of an interpersonal construct. *The Annual Review of Organizational Psychology and Organizational Behavior*, 1(1), 23–43. https:// doi .org/ 10 .1146/ annurev-orgpsych-031413-091305.

Gu, Q., Wang, G. G., & Wang, L. (2013). Social capital and innovation in R&D teams: The mediating roles of psychological safety and learning from mistakes. *R&D Management*, 43(2), 89–102. https://doi.org/10.1111/radm.12002.

Kahn, W. A. (1990). Psychological conditions of personal engagement and disengagement at work. *Academy of Management Journal*, 33(4), 692–724. https://doi.org/10.5465/256287.

Lee, J. Y., Swink, M., & Pandejpong, T. (2011). The roles of worker expertise, information sharing quality, and psychological safety in manufacturing process innovation: An intellectual capital perspective. *Production and Operations Management*, 20(4), 556–570. https://doi.org/10.1111/j.1937-5956.2010.01172.x

Leroy, H., Dierynck, B., Anseel, F., Simons, T., Halbesleben, J. R. B., & McCaughey, D. (2012). Behavioral integrity for safety, priority of safety, psychological safety, and patient safety: A team-level study. *Journal of Applied Psychology*, 97(6), 1273–1281. https://doi.org/10.1037/a0030076

Newman, A., Donohue, R., & Eva, N. (2017). Psychological safety: A systematic review of the literature. *Human Resource Management Review*, 27, 521–535. http://dx.doi.org/10.1016/j.hrmr.2017.01.001.

Palanski, M. E., & Vogelgesang, G. R. (2011). Virtuous creativity: The effects of leader behavioural integrity on follower creative thinking and risk taking. *Canadian*

Journal of Administrative Sciences/Revue Canadienne Des Sciences De l'Adminis-tration, 28(3), 259–269. https://doi.org/10.1002/cjas.219.

Schein, E. H., & Bennis, W. (1965). *Personal and Organizational Change through Group Methods*. Hoboken, NJ: Wiley.

Tynan, R. (2005). The effects of threat sensitivity and face giving on dyadic psychological safety and upward communication. *Journal of Applied Social Psychology*, 35(2), 223–247. https://doi.org/10.1111/j.1559-1816.2005.tb02119.x.

14. Organizational justice: in search of fairness and equity for your staff

TRIGGER

Reflecting on the different managerial jobs I have carried out, I do recall the moments, the events when organizational justice was at stake. In my own managerial role, I have sometimes caused feelings of injustice among my subordinates. However, it also happened that I became the victim of injustice myself. Especially when one is very loyal to an organization, it hurts a lot when one is being treated in an unfair way. I recall a meeting with my superior, in which I was hoping that my promotion to the next level would finally take place – a process which had already been going on for a while and for which the prospects looked very good. Therefore, in an optimistic state of mind, I entered at the agreed time the office of my superior. I could sense immediately that he was not in a very good mood, being a bit nervous, perspiring, face red, etc. In an elaborate and sometimes clumsy way, he started to explain why the promotion would not take place. During one of the last strategic meetings with the management team (of which I was part), I had opposed – also on behalf of my colleagues as being their spokesman –his plans for a reorganization to be carried out as we saw other possibilities. Based on my disagreement with his proposal, he considered me not to be loyal to the organization and perceived that as a reason for adjourning the decision for promotion. I was stupefied that having an argumentation, a difference of opinion about how to plan for downsizing our organization, was being perceived as disloyal and apparently a reason for withholding the approval of my promotion. I left the room, grabbed my car, drove to the seaside nearby the place where I was born, and walked the beach trying to find some relief and consolation for what had happened to me.

1. DEFINING THE CONCEPT

Aiming for a balanced approach, trying to achieve joint optimization both for performance and well-being, implies an important role for organizational justice. Organizational justice is made up of three components: distributive, procedural and interactional, which together can be considered to represent overall fairness (Ambrose & Arnaud, 2005). Distributive justice has to do with the justice of outcomes; procedural justice with the justice of the formal allocation process; and interactional justice has to do with the justice of interpersonal transactions/relationships with others (Cropanzano et al., 2007).

2.   FOUNDING FATHERS/MOTHERS

When asking around for the main authors in the field of organizational justice, academics working in the domains of I/O psychology, organizational behaviour and/or HR-Studies will almost automatically refer to the names of Jason Colquitt and Russell Cropanzano. Indeed, these are very important authors who have written oft-cited papers on organizational justice (see, for example, Colquitt, 2001, paper in *JAP* on dimensionality of organizational justice with 8,700+ citations, and Cropanzano and Mitchell, 2005 paper on social exchange theory in *JOM*, with 12,500+ citations). However, mentioning only these two names does not do justice to Jerald Greenberg's foundational work back in the 1980s (Greenberg, 1987) and 1990s (Greenberg, 1990). Going back even further, the seminal roots of organizational justice theory can be traced back to equity theory as developed by Adams (1965) in the 1960s. The popularity of the concept of organizational justice, both in practice as well as in theory, is huge. Google, in general, generates more than 300 million hits and Google Scholar more than 2.7 million hits.

Jason Colquitt is affiliated to the University of Georgia (USA) and Russell Cropanzano to the University of Colorado (USA).

3.   CONTENT OF THE THEORY

The focus of the theory is on how employees perceive and judge the way they are treated by their organization. Treated especially from an ethical and moral perspective, this will subsequently result in attitudinal and behavioural responses, such as satisfaction, trust, commitment, job performance, helping colleagues, customer satisfaction, and intention to leave. Paying attention to justice or fairness is thus very important for an organization and its line management as it has consequences for the quality of the employment relationship and its outcomes in terms of well-being and performance. Cropanzano et al. define organizational justice as 'a personal evaluation about the ethical and moral standing of managerial conduct' (2007, p. 35), which implies for managers the importance of taking on the perspective of an employee. For this reason, you will find below a set of questions which will help you to empathize with your employees in order to assess to what degree you have met their requirements for a just and fair employment relationship.

The roots of a theory of organizational justice stem from equity theory (Adams, 1965). The perception of equity (or inequity) is based on comparing inputs and outcomes. Input such as ideas, effort, knowledge, and service are compared with outcomes such as appreciation, pay, and status. Next to *equity,* Cropanzano et al. (2007, p. 37) also distinguish an allocation rule based on *equality* (providing each employee with roughly the same compensation) and an allocation rule based on *need* (in accordance with the most pressing needs of a person).

Initially, the concept of organizational justice was only focused on a fair distribution of the outcomes (distributive justice). Later on, procedural justice, defined as the perceived fairness of the process by which the outcomes are determined, was added to it (Cohen-Charash & Spector, 2001; Leventhal, 1980). Leventhal (1980) defined six normatively accepted principles, which once adhered to, would safeguard a decent degree of procedural fairness. These principles are: consistency, lack of bias, accurate information, representation of all stakeholders, possibility for appeal, and maintaining standards of professional conduct (see Table 14.1).

Next to procedures, we also have communication and the persons involved in that communication process, which gave rise to the third dimension of organizational justice being *interactional justice,* defined as how one person treats another. Based on a construct validation study, Colquitt (2001, also confirmed in a meta-analytic study, see Colquitt et al. (2001)) distinguishes two sub-dimensions of interactional justice. One is related to showing concern and respect with which one treats another. It is all about dignity and a decent treatment of the people involved and is called *interpersonal justice.* The other subdimension of interactional justice is called *informational justice* and refers to truthful, adequate information about the why and how of the procedures involved and how that has given rise to a certain distribution of the outcomes. So, *interpersonal* justice is focused on the people involved and the way they are treated, whereas *informational* justice is focused on providing adequate and reliable information about the procedures used. Table 14.1 (Cropanzano et al., 2007, p. 36) shows a systematic overview of the different dimensions of organizational justice.

4. EFFECTS/EMPIRICAL EVIDENCE

Making a distinction between the three dimensions of organizational justice (distributive, procedural, and interactional) is important as each dimension can have a different impact on attitude, behaviour, and related outcomes, as we will describe later on. At the same time, they do interact quite strongly – and that is fortunate. It implies that having an injustice distributive outcome can partially be compensated for with proper procedural justice and/or decent interactional

Table 14.1   Components of organizational justice

1. Distributive Justice: Appropriateness of outcomes. – Equity: Rewarding employees based on their contributions. – Equality: Providing each employee roughly the same compensation. – Need: Providing a benefit based on one's personal requirements.
2. Procedural Justice: Appropriateness of the allocation process. – Consistency: All employees are treated the same. – Lack of bias: No person or group is singled out for discrimination or ill-treatment. – Accuracy: Decisions are based on accurate information. – Representation of all concerned: Appropriate stakeholders have input into a decision. – Correction: There is an appeals process or other mechanism for fixing mistakes. – Ethics: Norms of professional conduct are not violated.
3. Interactional Justice: Appropriateness of the treatment one receives from authority figures. – Interpersonal justice: Treating an employee with dignity, courtesy, and respect. – Informational justice: Sharing relevant information with employees.

Note: Adapted from 'The management of organizational justice', by R. Cropanzano, D. E. Bowen, and S. W. Gilliland, 2007, Academy of Management Perspectives, 21, p. 36 (https://doi.org/10.5465/amp.2007.27895338). Copyright 2007 by Academy of Management.

justice. For example, a reorganization involving lay-offs and salary cuts can be perceived from a distributive perspective as unfair, yet making sure that the procedures are clear, correctly applied, inclusive of appeal procedures, and communicated in an exact and truthful way with respect and dignity for the people involved can make sure that overall the negative effects are not too dramatic.

Based on three meta-analytic reviews encompassing a whole range of studies, involving both field and laboratory studies (Cohen-Charash & Spector, 2001; Colquitt et al., 2001; Viswesvaran & Ones, 2002) we can conclude that the different dimensions of organizational justice link to a variety of outcomes such as trust, satisfaction, productivity, commitment, turnover and organizational citizenship behaviour (OCB[1]). Paying attention to organizational justice is thus not only required from a moral and ethical point of view (as a goal in itself), it also pays off as far as well-being of employees and their performance at work are concerned!

Making use of the overview by Cropanzano et al. (2007) and the meta-analysis of Cohen-Charash and Spector (2001), we present the following outcomes:

*   All three components of justice are quite strongly related to *trust*.
*   Perceived organizational justice relates to *affective commitment*, but according to Cohen-Charash and Spector (2001), the dimension of procedural justice is the best predictor.

- Justice also improves *performance in the job* as fairness improves, leading to strong interpersonal relationships and increased feelings of equity. As the attitude of the employee becomes more positive, it also motivates other employees to a higher level of job performance (Cropanzano et al., 2007; Karriker & Williams, 2007).
- All three forms of organizational justice are related to organizational citizenship behaviours,[2] inclusive of spillover effects to customer satisfaction and loyalty (Masterson, 2001; Maxham & Nettemeyer, 2003).
- Procedural and distributive justice are similarly related (negative relationship) to counterproductive work behaviour.
- General job satisfaction is similarly and relatively highly related to all three justice types (Cropanzano et al., 2007).

With respect to all kind of demographic variables, such as age, gender, ethnicity, and educational level, the meta-analyses indicate that apparently all people view justice in a similar way. However, this is still an area in need of further research according to Cropanzano et al. (2007).

5.   HRM AND A CLIMATE FOR JUSTICE

The above-mentioned important effects provide strong arguments for creating a *climate for justice* in the organization. Leadership and HRM practices can help to build that. Ways to do that can be found in Cropanzano et al. (2007). Their paper discusses possibilities from the domain of HRM such as selection, reward systems, conflict management, layoffs/reorganizations, and performance management/appraisal systems – I highly recommended further reading.

By way of summary and overview, Figure 14.1 presents below the framework of Cohen-Charash and Spector (2001, p. 283) for the antecedents and outcomes of organizational justice.

6.   REFLECTIVE QUESTIONS

The different dimensions and concepts of organizational justice have been extensively tested and validated in empirical research. Below we present for every dimension the kind of questions that have been used to measure the perception among *employees*. In other words: how did they experience a specific dimension of organizational justice by Colquitt, 2001 (p. 389). Each set of items is followed by a set of reflective questions (developed by J. Paauwe) for the *line manager* in charge, in order to assess whether he or she did a good job in shaping the employment relationship in such a way that the different dimensions of organizational justice have been met.

124   *Progressing performance and well-being at work*

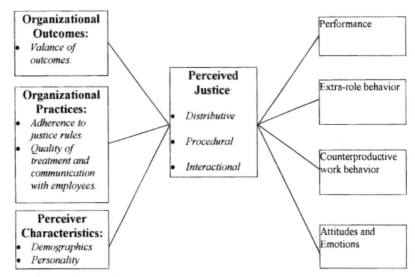

Note: Reprinted from 'The role of justice in organizations: A meta-analysis', by Y. Cohen-Charash and P. E. Spector, 2001, Organizational Behavior and Human Decision Processes, 86(2), p. 283 (https://doi.org/10.1006/obhd.2001.2958). Copyright 2001 by Academic Press.

Figure 14.1   Justice in organizations

Distributive Justice: Self-assessment Items

The following items refer to your outcomes (such as pay, appreciation, status, promotion, etc.). To what extent:

- Does your outcome reflect the effort you have put into your work?
- Is your outcome appropriate for the work you have completed?
- Does your outcome reflect what you have contributed to the organization?
- Is your outcome justified, given your performance?

Distributive Justice: Reflective Questions for the Supervisor/Manager

- In distributing the outcomes (in terms of pay, promotion, status, feedback, appreciation), to what degree did you do a just and fair job for every person in your team/department?
- In comparing the employees in your team/department, to what degree did you do a fair job in ranking them related to their performance/contribution?

Procedural Justice: Self-assessment Items

The following items refer to the procedures used to arrive at your outcome. To what extent:

- Have you been able to *express your views and feelings* during those procedures?
- Have you had *influence* over the outcome arrived at by those procedures?
- Have these procedures been applied *consistently?*
- Have these procedures been *free of bias?*
- Have these procedures been based on *accurate information*?
- Have you been able to *appeal* the outcome arrived at by those procedures?
- Have these procedures upheld ethical and moral standards?

Procedural Justice: Reflective Questions for the Supervisor/Manager

- To what degree did you allow for – or, even better, stimulate – a two-sided conversation with your employee?
- Did you apply the procedures consistently across the employees reporting to you?
- Did you do a thorough job in collecting adequate information which would warrant the kind of decisions you took for distributing the outcomes in a just and fair way?

Interactional Justice

This dimension has been split up into *interpersonal justice* (implying that one treats an employee with dignity, courtesy, and respect) and *informational justice* (meaning that one shares relevant information with employees) (following Colquitt, 2001 in *JAP*).

Interpersonal Justice: Self-assessment Items, Which Refer to the Authority Figure who Enacted the Procedure

To what extent:

- Has he/she treated you in a polite manner?
- Has he/she treated you with dignity?
- Has he/she treated you with respect?
- Has he/she refrained from improper remarks or comments?

Interpersonal Justice: Reflective Question for the Supervisor/Manager

- Treating an employee with dignity, courtesy and respect is part of interpersonal justice. Can you safely and honestly conclude that your behaviour towards your employee did indeed meet with those standards?

Informational Justice: Self-Assessment Items, Which Refer to Providing Adequate and Reliable Information about the Procedures Used

To what extent:

- Has he/she been candid in his/her communication with you?
- Has he/she explained the procedures thoroughly?
- Were his/her explanations regarding the procedures reasonable?
- Has he/she communicated details in a timely manner?
- Has he/she seemed to tailor his/her communications to individual's specific needs?

Informational Justice: Reflective Question for the Supervisor/Manager

- Sharing relevant information in a *thorough, candid, and timely way* is all part of informational justice. Looking back upon the applied procedures and the interactions involved, can you safely and honestly conclude that the information provided to and shared with your employees did indeed meet with those standards?

These kinds of questions and answers will help to assess the degree to which you – as a manager – have met the requirements of your employees and workers for a just and fair employment relationship.

This will serve as a prelude or stepping stone for the next cycle, in which we again travel the loop of why HRM is as it is, why HR practices work (or not), develop stronger meaningful (work) situations, offer an ever resource-richer work environment, and then once more reflect on what we have achieved.

NOTE

1. Organizational citizenship behaviours (OCBs) are employee behaviours that go beyond the call of duty (Organ, 1988).

REFERENCES

Adams, J. S. (1965). Inequity in social exchange. *Advances in Experimental Social Psychology*, 2, 267–299.

Ambrose, M. L., & Arnaud, A. (2005). Distributive and procedural justice: Construct distinctiveness, construct interdependence, and overall justice. In J. Greenberg & J. Colquitt (eds), *The Handbook of Organizational Justice* (pp. 59–84). Mahwah, NJ: Erlbaum.

Cohen-Charash, Y., & Spector, P. E. (2001). The role of justice in organizations: A meta-analysis. *Organizational Behavior and Human Decision Processes*, 86(2), 278–321. https://doi.org/10.1006/obhd.2001.2958.

Colquitt, J. A. (2001). On the dimension of organizational justice: A construct validation of a measure. *Journal of Applied Psychology*, 86(3), 386–400. doi:10.1037//0021-9010.86.3.386.

Colquitt, J. A., Conlon, D. E., Wesson, M. J., Porter, C. O. L. H., & Ng, K. Y. (2001). Justice at the millennium: A meta-analytic review of 25 years of organizational justice research. *Journal of Applied Psychology*, 86(3), 425–445. Retrieved from https://psycnet.apa.org/doi/10.1037/0021-9010.86.3.425.

Cropanzano, R., & Mitchell, M. S. (2005). Social exchange theory: An interdisciplinary review. *Journal of Management*, 31(6), 874–900. https://doi.org/10.1177%2F0149206305279602.

Cropanzano, R., Bowen, D. E., & Gilliland, S. W. (2007). The management of organizational justice. *Academy of Management Perspectives*, 21(4), 34–48. https://doi.org/10.5465/amp.2007.27895338.

Greenberg, J. (1987). A taxonomy of organizational justice theories. *Academy of Management Review*, 12(1), 9–22. https://doi.org/10.5465/amr.1987.4306437.

Greenberg, J. (1990). Organizational justice: Yesterday, today, and tomorrow. *Journal of Management*, 16(2), 399–432.

Heider, F. (1958). *The Psychology of Interpersonal Relations*. New York: Wiley.

Homans, G. C. (1974). *Social Behavior: Its Elementary Forms. New York: Harcourt Brac.

Karriker, J. H. , & Williams, M. L. (2007). Organizational justice and organizational citizenship behaviour: A mediated multifoci model. *Journal of Management*, 35(1), 112–135. https://doi.org/10.1177%2F0149206307309265.

Leventhal, G. S. (1980). What should be done with equity theory? New approaches to the study of justice in social relationships. In K. Gergen, M. Greenberg, & R. Willis (eds), *Social Exchange: Advances in Experimental and Social Psychology* (pp. 27–55). New York: Plenum.

Masterson, S. S. (2001). A trickle-down model of organizational justice: Relating employees' and customers' perceptions of and reactions to fairness. *Journal of Applied Psychology*, 88, 594–604. Retrieved from https://psycnet.apa.org/doi/10.1037/0021-9010.86.4.594.

Maxham, J. G., & Netemyer, R. G. (2003). Firms reap what they sow: The effects of shared values and perceived organizational justice on customers' evaluations of complaint handling. *Journal of Marketing*, 67(1), 46–62. https://doi.org/10.1509%2Fjmkg.67.1.46.18591.

Organ, D. W. (1988). *Organizational Citizenship Behavior*. Lexington, MA: Lexington Books.

Visweswaran, C., & Ones, D. S. (2002). Examining the construct of organizational justice: A meta-analytic evaluation of relations with work attitudes and behaviors. *Journal of Business Ethics*, 38(3), 193–203.

15. Social determination theory: how it can help to do a good job as a manager

TRIGGER

For several years, during the Christmas break and just preceding New Year's Eve, I have written a letter to the people in my department – a letter which would accompany their Christmas gift. In my writing, I would reflect on important events in the year gone by, indicating highlights and achievements, and thanking the members of staff for all their hard work, their fellowship, and the results achieved. Looking back on the past year in such a way, it was undoubtedly accompanied by some thoughts about my own 'leadership' role and style. Did I stimulate people enough? Did I pay enough attention to their personal needs and issues? Did I listen carefully enough to what people had to say or was I just too busy? Most importantly, did I do justice to their needs and feelings of fairness? This is not always an easy and comfortable exercise, especially in times of reorganization and downsizing, tough decisions are not always experienced as fair.

1.   DEFINING THE CONCEPT AND HOW IT CAN HELP PRACTITIONERS

Starting from the premise that people display a natural process of self-motivation for growth and development, the social-contextual setting can facilitate or hinder this process. That's why, in reality, we meet with both pro-active and engaged people as well as with passive and alienated people. To enable intrinsic motivation, growth, and well-being, three innate basic psychological needs – *competence (mastery), relatedness (belonging), and autonomy* – must be satisfied. If not, it will result in diminished motivation and well-being. The social determination theory has found its applications in a variety of domains, among which is the world of work, where intrinsic motivation, growth, and well-being are a crucial part of the employment relationship people have with their work. The way in which work is organized, the behaviour of managers and colleagues, leadership style, and culture are all very important and influential for creating a context in which these basic needs are being thwarted or nourished.

2.   FOUNDING FATHERS/MOTHERS

Very often a theory or approach has different fathers and mothers. However, for those familiar with social determination theory there are only two incontestable fathers: Richard M. Ryan and Edward L. Deci, psychologists who have spent almost their whole life on the topic of motivation, developing ideas, and testing these by carrying out numerous lab experiments, which finally culminated in their social determination theory – a theory about motivation, learning and development. Since its conception, the theory has been applied in numerous domains such as applied psychology/clinical settings, sports, nursing and health care, education (interaction patterns between parents and children), and work motivation. The popularity of their theorizing is evident. On Google Scholar, Richard M. Ryan generates more than 550,000 citations, whereas Edward L. Deci has more than 480,000 citations. This might also have to do with the attractiveness of their ideas and the usability of them in the increasingly more popular stream of 'positive' psychology across the globe. Both are linked to the University of Rochester, Rochester New York State (USA) as well as to the Institute for Positive Psychology & Education, Australian Catholic University, Sydney (Australia).

3.   OVERVIEW OF THE THEORY/CONTENT

Based on the familiar distinction between extrinsic motivation (based on rewards and punishment, grading systems, compliance) and intrinsic motivation (out of pure interest, enjoyment, based on core values and morality), Ryan and Deci (2000) identify three basic needs, which they consider to be innate and universalistic across the globe:

- *Competence*: the need to build competence and gain mastery over tasks which are important to people.
- *Connection or relatedness*: the need to have close relationships, to be connected, and to have a sense of belonging.
- *Autonomy*: the need to be in control of your own life, of your own behaviour, and to be a master of your destiny.

These three needs motivate the individual to engage in certain behaviours and specify nutriments and resources that are essential for psychological health, growth, and well-being. The very fact that these needs are universal and innate does not imply that they cannot express themselves differently dependent upon culture, time, or previous experience. If all three needs are met, people are considered to be self-determined, however this requires continuous sustenance, for which a supportive environment is crucial (Ryan & Deci, 2000). That is why they labelled their approach *social* determination theory (SDT). As far as resources or nutriments (the specific term used by Ryan and Deci) are concerned, we can think of social support, offering challenges, training, and development opportunities, getting constructive feedback, etc.

4.   APPLICATIONS FOR PRACTICE: SDT AND THE WORLD OF WORK

At work people will encounter a variety of sources for motivation. These can be extrinsic such as pay, status, and approval by others, or intrinsic as it enables mastery, competence, or gaining satisfaction from the activity itself without the need for appreciation from others. So, as employees and workers, we find ourselves amidst both extrinsic and intrinsic stimuli, which lead to self-determined and non-self-determined behaviours (Ackerman, 2019). Purely self-determined behaviours are intrinsically driven (out of joy, sheer interest in the action itself, and the kind of satisfaction it generates). How do we recognize somebody who is a self-determined individual? According to Ackerman (2019), it is most likely somebody who:

- believes she/he is in control of her own life;
- takes responsibility for her own behaviour, taking both the credit as well as the blame;
- is self-motivated instead of driven by the standard of others or external sources;
- determines her actions based on her own internal values and goals.

According to SDT, functioning in this way can be considered as the optimal outcome and implies that a person '... engages in an activity or behavior with volition, enthusiasm, positive affect and energy' (Gagné & Vansteenkiste, 2013, p. 63).

Based on lab experiments, Ryan and Deci found that with respect to *goal-setting*, workers/employees are more successful when they are able to set and pursue their goals in their own way instead of being highly regulated or set by a strict external system. As far as the relationship between goals and subsequent success is concerned, research indicates that success is more likely when the goals are related to intrinsic motives and intended to satisfy basic needs.

With respect to the role of supervisors, Koestner and Hope (2014) found that success in goal achievement is more likely when workers are supported by empathetic and supportive people instead of controlling or directive people (Ackerman, 2019).

Based on research by Gagné and Deci (2005), a supervisor or manager needs to be careful with distributing *extrinsic* rewards as they run the risk that this will reduce the already present *intrinsic* motivation. This requires a careful balancing act as too few extrinsic rewards might lead to feelings among workers of not being appreciated or recognized, whereas too many might endanger the positive effect of already present *intrinsic* motivation.

The role of a manager in supporting the degree of autonomy of a worker is also important as it will stimulate job satisfaction, positive performance evaluations, psychological adjustment, and acceptance of organizational change. Especially important for the interpersonal style of the manager is to be trained in understanding the perspective of the worker, while encouraging his/her initiative-taking and providing feedback, not in a controlling way, but in a way which supports the employee's autonomy. This will help employees to become more trusting of the organization and will generate the kind of positive work-related attitudes as mentioned above (Gagné & Deci, 2005).

In this respect, Bakker and van Woerkom (2017) hint more specifically at the importance of transformational leadership as being conducive in stimulating the basic needs of competence, relatedness, and autonomy. Providing feedback, ensuring that the job fits the abilities of the employee, and allowing for a sufficient degree of autonomy and control in the job will further the needs of competence and autonomy (Bakker & van Woerkom, 2017; Hetland et al., 2015). With respect to meeting the need of relatedness, Breevaart et al. (2014; 2015) mention the importance of providing personal attention and social support.

5. REFLECTIVE QUESTIONS

From a reflective point of view, it is important to check whether the three basic needs of your employees have been met and, if so, to what degree. In Table 15.1 below, we give an overview of the questions/items which have been used in empirical research to assess among participants the degree to which the three basic needs were being covered (Van den Broeck et al., 2010, p. 1002). Each set of items is followed by a set of reflective questions (developed by J. Paauwe) for the line manager in charge, in order to assess whether he or she did a good job in shaping the employment relationship in such a way that the three basic needs have been met.

From the perspective of motivating your employees and workers, this set of questions and answers will help you to assess whether you as a manager did a good job in shaping the employment relationship in such a way that the three basic needs have been met.

Just like the preceding chapter, this will serve as a stepping stone for the next cycle, in which we again travel the loop of why HRM is as it is, why HR practices work (or not), developing stronger meaningful (work) situations, offering an ever resource-richer work environment, and then once more reflecting on what we have achieved.

Table 15.1   Capturing autonomy, competence, and relatedness at work

---

Need for competence: self-assessment items

– I don't really feel competent in my job (R)* .46
– I really master my tasks at my job .60
– I feel competent at my job .70
– I doubt whether I am able to execute my job properly (R)* .56
– I am good at the things I do in my job .66
– I have the feeling that I can even accomplish the most difficult tasks at work .59

Need for competence: reflective questions for the supervisor/manager

– To what degree did I *stimulate* my employee to develop him/herself?
– Did I *compliment* my employee for having achieved mastery in his/her job?
– To what degree did I offer *support* to my employee for *boosting* his/her self-confidence?
– Did I offer enough *challenges* in the job my employee is currently doing?
– To what degree did I offer enough *support* to my employee for overcoming his/her doubts in carrying out the job?

Need for relatedness: self-assessment items

– I don't really feel connected with other people at my job (R) .65
– At work, I feel part of a group .63
– I don't really mix with other people at my job (R) .63
– At work, I can talk with people about things that really matter to me .63
– I often feel alone when I am with my colleagues (R) .59
– At work, people involve me in social activities* .44
– At work, there are people who really understand me* .60
– Some people I work with are close friends of mine .63
– At work, no one cares about me (R)* .59
– There is nobody I can share my thoughts with if I would want to do so (R)* .49

Need for relatedness: reflective questions for the supervisor/manager

– What did I do to make sure that my employees are well *integrated* into their team/department?
– Did I pay enough attention to *signals* that someone might be a 'loner'?
– When having a break or an informal gathering, do people/your employees feel free to *express* themselves?
– Did you manage to develop a *trusting relationship* with your employees/those who report directly to you (or is your relationship with them more based on a command and control style)?

Need for autonomy: self-assessment items

– I feel free to express my ideas and opinions in this job* .59
– I feel like I can be myself at my job .69
– At work, I often feel like I have to follow other people's commands (R) .61
– If I could choose, I would do things at work differently (R) .57
– The tasks I have to do at work are in line with what I really want to do .61
– I feel free to do my job the way I think it could best be done .59
– In my job, I feel forced to do things I do not want to do (R) .54

Need for autonomy: reflective questions for the supervisor/manager

– Do you give enough leeway for employees to sort out themselves how they want to carry out the job assigned to them?
– To what degree are your department and the tasks that need to be carried out subject to 'micro-management'?
– Are the kinds of tasks people carry out in your department aligned with their passion?
– To what degree is your leadership style characterized by supporting and respecting the autonomy of your employees (or is the reverse the case: a nosy, nitpicking style of leadership)?

Note: (R) Reversed item. *Item *not* included in the final scale. The current study reports on the Dutch version of the W-BNS, the validity of the English version remains to be studied. The items were translated using the translation/back-translation procedure. The French version of the W-BNS is available upon request from the corresponding author. Adapted from 'Capturing autonomy, competence, and relatedness at work: Construction and initial validation of the Work-related Basic Need Satisfaction scale', by A. Van den Broeck, M. Vansteenkiste, H. De Witte, B. Soenens, and W. Lens, 2010, *Journal of Occupational and Organizational Psychology*, 83, p. 1002 (https://doi.org/10.1348/096317909X481382). Copyright 2010 by The British Psychological Society.

REFERENCES

Ackerman, C. E. (2019, June 21). *Self Determination Theory and How It Explains Motivation.* Positive Psychology.com. https:// positivepsychology .com/ self -determination-theory/.

Bakker, A. B., & van Woerkom, M. (2017). Flow at work: A self-determination perspective. *Occupational Health Science*, 1, 47–65. https:// doi .org/ 10.1007/ s41542 -017-0003-3.

Breevaart, K., Bakker, A. B., Demerouti, E., Sleebos, D. M., & Maduro, V. (2015). Uncovering the underlying relationship between transformational leaders and followers' task performance. *Journal of Personnel Psychology*, 13, 194–203. https:// doi.org/10.1027/1866-5888/a000118.

Breevaart, K., Bakker, A. B., Hetland, J., Demerouti, E., Olsen, O. K., & Espevik, R. (2014). Daily transactional and transformational leadership and daily employee engagement. *Journal of Occupational and Organizational Psychology*, 87(1), 138–157. https://doi.org/10.1111/joop.12041.

Gagné, M., & Deci, E. L. (2005). Self-determination theory and work motivation. *Journal of Organizational Behavior*, 26(4), 331–362. https:// doi .org/ 10.1002/job .322.

Gagné, M., & Vansteenkiste, M. (2013). Self-determination theory's contribution to positive organizational psychology. In A.B. Bakker (ed.), *Advances in Positive Organizational Psychology* (pp. 61–82). Leeds: Emerald.

Hetland, J., Hetland, H., Bakker, A. B., Demerouti, E., Andreassen, C. S., & Pallesen, S. (2015). Psychological need fulfillment as a mediator of the relationship between transformational leadership and positive job attitudes. *Career Development International*, 20, 464–481. http://dx.doi.org/10.1108/CDI-10-2014-0136.

Koestner, R., & Hope, N. (2014). A self-determination theory approach to goals. In M. Gagné (ed.), *The Oxford Handbook of Work Engagement, Motivation, and Self-determination Theory* (pp. 400–413). Oxford: Oxford University Press.

Ryan, R. M., & Deci, E. L. (2000). Self-determination theory and the facilitation of intrinsic motivation, social development, and well-being. *American Psychologist*, 55(1), 58–78. https://doi.org/10.1037/0003-066X.55.1.68.

Van den Broeck, A., Vansteenkiste, M., De Witte, H., Soenens, B., & Lens, W. (2010). Capturing autonomy, competence, and relatedness at work: Construction and initial validation of the work-related basic need satisfaction scale. *Journal of Occupational and Organizational Psychology*, 83, 981–1002. https:// doi .org/ 10 .1348/096317909X481382.

Appendix: Evidence-based management – meaning and implications for practitioners

INTRODUCTION

In the preface and introductory chapter of this book, we referred to proven theories and HRM practices. What do we mean by 'proven'? As far as HR practices are concerned, we can equalize 'proven' with 'tested'. By conducting empirical research, the effectiveness of an HR practice (for example, that cognitive ability tests as a selection device are a good predictor of performance in the job) can be established.

With respect to so-called proven theories, this is a slightly different ballgame. Some theoretical frameworks such as goal-setting theory, strength of the system theory, and job demands resource theory, have been properly tested for by means of collecting and analysing empirical data. Some of these theories/approaches have also been subject to systematic reviews (inclusive meta-analyses) and have achieved an undisputable status as thoroughly tested. Goal-setting theory is a good example in this respect. Other theories or theoretical frameworks have been used a lot – both in practice as well as in theory – because of their high face validity. By this we mean that a theory appears or seems to measure/reflect what it intends to measure or represent in the empirical reality. The schematic representation in a theoretical framework is appealing to the reader, however it has not (yet) been properly tested for. A good example of this is the so-called contextually-based human resource theory (Paauwe, 2004), which has been used quite frequently, but has only been partially tested.

The emphasis on proven or tested OB and HR interventions and related theories has been stimulated by the Evidence Based Management (EBM) movement. Initiated in 2006 by Denise Rousseau, who later worked together with Bob Briner, they together initiated the Center for Evidence-Based Management (www.cebma.org).

EVIDENCE-BASED MANAGEMENT AND BACKGROUND

In a presidential address to the Academy of Management, Rousseau makes a strong plea for improving management practice by making use of evidence-based management, which implies that one '... derives principles from research evidence and translates them into practices that solve organizational problems' (2006, p. 256). In this way, evidence-based management can help to better achieve organizational goals to the benefit of all who are involved, such as employees, shareholders, and the public in general. However, according to Rousseau, reality is different, as research findings apparently do not find their way to the workplace and managers prefer to rely on experience and the consulting of colleagues rather than on systematic knowledge as generated by sound academic research. This leads to the conclusion of a research–practice gap. One of the ways to close this gap is through evidence-based management. In some other fields (such as medicine), evidence-based practice has already become common.

As HRM is also part of management in general, it is worth taking a closer look at whether the domain of HRM also suffers from a research-practice gap. Based on a survey among 5,000 HR professionals, Rynes et al. (2002) found that there are large discrepancies between established research findings (for example, most people over-evaluate how well they perform on the job) and what HR practitioners believe to be true. The survey was composed of 35 topics which covered the majority of the dimensions of the Human Resource Certification Institute's exam (professional in HRM). For each topic, the available academic evidence was checked and in this way a number of both false and true statements were included. Subsequently respondents were asked to indicate whether they agreed/disagreed or were uncertain about the proper answer (Rynes et al., 2002, p. 151). The average respondent answered a bit more than half of all items in a correct way, yet there was a lot of variation among the respondents agreeing with particular items. Some items scored a low 16–18%, whereas others received a high 94–96% agreement. With respect to ways of seeking information, practitioners mainly rely on other HR professionals in the same organization, the SHRM website, and other internet sites. As far as journals and magazines are concerned, they do read HR magazine and very few respondents (less than 1%) indicated that they read research-orientated journals such as *Journal of Applied Psychology, Personnel Psychology,* and *Academy of Management Journal* (Rynes et al., 2002, p. 161). However, they do indicate that they wished they had more time to read academic journals. Finally, HR managers having a higher job level, reading relatively more academic literature, and having an SPHR certificate, agree on average more with the academic research findings (Rynes et al., 2002, p. 163).

The study has been replicated in the Netherlands by Sanders et al. (2008) using 25 of the 35 items, and leaving out some of the items from the original survey (for example, with respect to compensation and benefits) as being less applicable in a Dutch setting. As far as the outcomes are concerned, there was a mean score of 62% of correct answers (compare: Rynes et al. (2002) survey 57%) and just like in the USA-based survey, a lot of variation in the degree of agreement among the Dutch respondents (Sanders et al., 2008, p. 1981). With respect to seeking information, the Dutch sample also gives preference to professional journals over academic journals and also indicates a reliance on other HR professionals and websites in their search process for information.

What we can conclude is that amidst the general management profession, HR managers are apparently not excluded from being part of the research-practice gap. We can, of course, mention a dozen reasons why this is the case (such as being too busy; no time to read; academics writing in a way which is difficult to read; academics not taking the trouble to publish their findings in easy accessible professional journals, etc.), but better to pay attention to how we can reverse the trend of a too large group of HR professionals not making use of all the systematic evidence there is available. In this respect we can benefit from all the efforts that have taken place to promote evidence-based practice by people such as Rousseau and Briner, and many of their colleagues. They have established, as already indicated above, the Center for Evidence-Based Management (www.cebma.org). Based on numerous papers published by this center, we describe how to become an evidence-based HR practitioner or line manager.

FROM CONCEPT TO PRACTICE

Evidence-based management, in short, derives principles from research evidence and translates these into practices that solve organizational problems (Rousseau, 2006, p. 256). Based on Sackett et al., 1997), evidence-based practice is about integrating individual practitioner expertise with the best available external evidence from systematic research in making decisions about how to deal with problems and issues (Briner, 2007, p. 3). It is about making decisions '… through the conscious, explicit and judicious use of the best available evidence from multiple sources' (Barends et al., 2014):

- *A critical evaluation of the best possible research evidence*: findings from empirical studies published in academic journals with a special focus on systematic reviews, including meta-analyses.[1]

- *Practitioner expertise and judgement*: the practitioner with his/her professional expertise combined with the insights of colleagues, (line) managers, and consultants.
- *Evidence from the local context*: the organization itself is an important source for data, whether it be financial data, data from customers or clients, or data concerning employees, such as turnover, satisfaction, and engagement data stemming from employee engagement surveys.
- *The values and concerns of people who might be affected by the decision*: in this respect we can distinguish internal stakeholders, such as employees, the different layers of management and external stakeholders such as clients, customers, shareholders, and the public at large. Based on their views and values, they will react differently to the possible consequences of the organizations' decisions. So, it is important to anticipate these diverging reactions both from inside as well as from outside the organization (text based on Barends et al. (2014), which is also shown below in Figure A1 by the Center for Evidence-Based Management (2011)[2]).

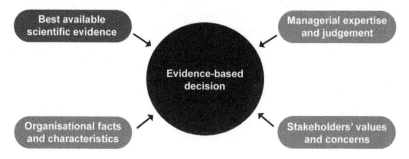

Note: Reprinted from the Center for Evidence-Based Management (CEBMa), 2011 (https://cebma.org/).

Figure A1   The evidence-based management (EBM) approach

The whole practice of evidence-based decision making demonstrates that focusing on the importance of scientific evidence does not exclude the professional expertise of the practitioner him/herself. On the contrary, he/she is of vital importance, nor does it exclude the values and concerns of those who will be affected by subsequent decisions. Actually, evidence-based practice is a form of embedded decision making. 'Embedded' because it is not only based on professional expertise in combination with the best available academic evidence, but also takes into account internal and external stakeholders and the specific context and related data/characteristics of the organization.

The example below in Figure A2 (Briner, 2019, p. 4; based on the issue of low engagement among employees) shows the kind of questions to be asked using the four sources:

Source	Sample questions asked to gather evidence to help identify the *problem* of low employee engagement (EE)
Scientific literature/ findings	• What do scientific findings suggest are the problems with low EE? • How valid and reliable is our measure of EE? • What do the results of scientific studies tell us about the *effects* of low EE? In what ways might this be a problem or lead to problems? How strong are these effects? • What do the results of scientific studies tell us about the *causes* of low EE? Are these causes amenable to intervention and change? • What theories have been used to explain low EE? • How trustworthy and relevant is this information?
Organizational data	• What do organizational data tell us about the nature of the low EE problem? How much of a problem is it? • What are the numbers? Are there any trends or changes over time? Are there patterns relating to particular parts of the organization or roles or functions? • Do organizational data reveal anything about the effects of low EE? What problems is it causing? • Do organizational data reveal anything about the causes of low EE? • How trustworthy and relevant is this information?
Stakeholders' concerns	• What do stakeholders (e.g., employees, managers, customers, clients, trade unions, shareholders, etc.) believe are the problems with low EE? • Do stakeholders have views about the possible *effects* of low EE? • What are stakeholders' perceptions of possible *causes* of low EE? • How trustworthy and relevant is this information?
Professional expertise	• Based on our experiences and expertise, what do we think is the nature of the problem of low EE? • From our experience what are the *effects* of low EE? • What do we believe, from our experience, are the *causes* of low EE? • Drawing on our expertise, what are our theories about the causes of low EE? • How trustworthy and relevant is this information?

Note: Reprinted from 'The basics of evidence-based practice', by R. Briner, 2019, HR People + Strategy SHRM, p. 4 (https://www.hrps.org/resources/people-strategy-journal/ Winter2019/Pages/EBP-briner.aspx).

Figure A2   *Sample questions related to the issue of low employee engagement (EE)*

According to Briner (2019, p. 6), using the four sources, as indicated above, requires a structured approach as follows:

1. Asking: Translating a practical issue or problem into an answerable question.
2. Acquiring: Systematically searching and retrieving the evidence.

3.   Appraising: Critically judging the trustworthiness and relevance of the evidence.
4.   Aggregating: Weighing and pulling together the evidence.
5.   Applying: Incorporating the evidence into the decision-making process.
6.   Assessing: Evaluating the outcome of the decision taken.

For further information, useful papers, etc., we refer to the site of the Center for Evidence-Based Management (www.cebma.org). In relation to the chapters presented in this book, giving concise systematic academic evidence for the usefulness of a selected set of 'proven' theories and 'tested' HR practices, the reader should be aware that we in this way only present *one out of the four* required sources as depicted in Figure A1. For those who want to fully immerse themselves into evidence-based HRM, we refer to Kroon (2021).

NOTES

1.   'A systematic review identifies as fully as possible all the scientific studies of relevance to a particular subject and then assesses the validity of the evidence of each study separately before interpreting the full body of evidence. One especially prevalent form of systematic review is a meta-analysis. It is a study of studies, where findings across studies are combined statistically in order to achieve a more accurate estimate of the results and the strength of effects that are described in the various studies (Rousseau & Barends, 2011, p. 229)'.
2.   https://cebma.org/.

REFERENCES

Barends, E., Rousseau, D. M., & Briner, R. B. (2014). Evidence-based management: The basic principles. *Centre for Evidence-Based Management.* https://www.cebma.org/wp-content/uploads/Evidence-Based-Practice-The-Basic-Principles.pdf.
Briner, R. (2007). Is HRM evidence-based and does it matter. *Institute of Employment Studies Opinion Paper OP6*, 1–7. https://cebma.org/wp-content/uploads/Briner-Is-HRM-evidence-based-and-does-it-matter.pdf.
Briner, R. (2019). The basics of evidence-based practice. *HR People + Strategy SHRM*, 1–7. https://www.hrps.org/resources/people-strategy-journal/Winter2019/Pages/EBP-briner.aspx.
Kroon, B. (2021). *Evidence Based HRM. What (Do) We Know About People in Workplaces?* The Netherlands: Wolf Publishers.
Paauwe, J. (2004). *HRM and Performance: Achieving Long-term Viability.* Oxford: Oxford University Press Inc.
Rousseau, D. M. (2006). Is there such a thing as "evidence-based management"? *Academy of Management Review*, 31(2), 256–269. https://doi.org/10.5465/amr.2006.20208679.

Rousseau, D. M., & Barends, E. G. (2011). Becoming an evidence-based HR practitioner. *Human Resource Management Journal*, 21(3), 221–235. https://doi.org/10.1111/j.1748-8583.2011.00173.x

Rynes, S. L., Colbert, A. E., & Brown, K. G. (2002). HR professionals' beliefs about effective human resource practices: Correspondence between research and practice. *Human Resource Management: Advancing Human Resource Research and Practice*, 41(2),149–174. https://doi.org/10.1002/hrm.10029.

Sanders, K., van Riemsdijk, M., & Groen, B. (2008). The gap between research and practice: A replication study on the HR professionals' beliefs about effective human resource practices. *The International Journal of Human Resource Management*, 19(10), 1976–1988. https://doi.org/10.1080/09585190802324304.

Index